The Digital Decluttering Workbook

How to Succeed with Digital Minimalism, Defeat Smartphone Addiction, Detox Social Media, and Organize Your Online Life

By Alex Wong

https://alexwongpublishing.com/

Table Of Contents

Related books

The Art of Decluttering and Organizing

How to Tidy Up your Home, Stop Clutter, and Simplify your Life (Without Going Crazy)

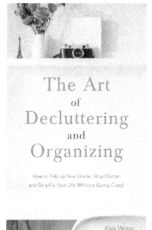

With real, actionable advice, *The Art of Decluttering and Organizing* is a decluttering workbook designed to help you prioritize your possessions, shift your mindset away from consumerism, and make the sometimes tough decisions that will help you on your journey to a more fulfilling life. **Get it now!**

https://bit.ly/artofdecluttering1

The Decluttering Your Life Workbook

The Secrets of Organizing Your Home, Mind, Health, Finances, and Relationships in 6 Easy Steps

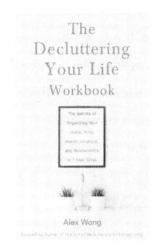

With a targeted blueprint for overhauling your entire lifestyle, the *Decluttering Your Life Workbook* arms you with all the knowledge you need to start creating lifelong positive change and setting yourself up for success! Don't put up with a hectic and chaotic lifestyle for any longer. Now you can calm your mind, cut back on clutter, and see the benefits of minimalism first-hand. **Start decluttering your life now!**

https://bit.ly/declutteryourlife1

Introduction

"Social media shows us a very unrealistic face of everything. It makes you feel that you have thousands of friends when in reality, you don't."

- Dr. Prem Jagyasi

My name is Alex Wong. If you're reading this, chances are that you are interested in de-cluttering your digital life. Perhaps you spend too much time on social media, and have trouble making time for more important things in life. Perhaps you find it difficult to be productive with all of your digital devices, and you want an action plan for reorganizing your digital life.

Either way, you've made the first step by picking up this book. After living as a digital nomad for a number of years, I've learned a large number of tips, tricks, guidelines, and exercises for maintaining an organized digital life. Since seeing how much of a big difference this made in my life, I want to give this ability to others, so they can take control of their digital lives like I did.

I was born in the 1980s, and I grew up in the 90's and

early 2000's. Being born during this period gave me the opportunity to see how life was before the internet and smartphones. Many people who already had these things growing up don't truly realize how much these things have revolutionized our lives.

I remember getting my first desktop computer when I was about 16 years old, well after most people get their first smartphones these days. This computer was *huge*, and bulky with a monitor, hard drive, printer, and scanner. To me at the time, it was one of the most amazing things I had ever seen. I remember the first time I ever connected to the internet like it was yesterday.

Of course, the internet at the time required usage of the phone line, which would take a number of minutes just to connect in the first place. If anybody tried to call your line while you were connected, they would get a busy signal. If somebody on your end tried to use the phone, they could even end up kicking you off the internet by accident!

Once you actually got connected, the speed wasn't anything to write home about. It was nowhere near as fast as 4G, 3G, or even 2G for that matter! It would often take you over 20 minutes to download a simple mp3 file, and forget about downloading movies! Of course, to me at the time, the technology was quite revolutionary. I can't imagine how much fast 5G will change the world as we know it.

Fast forward to my college days, when I received my first cell phone. This was another game changer. Of course, this was still before the first iPhone came out, so it was hardly anything like the smartphones we have nowadays. My first phone was a Sony Ericsson given to me by my sister. It had actual buttons on it, and the screen wasn't more than 1-2 inches. Eventually, I got my own smartphone when I was teaching in Busan, Korea years later. The smartphone made a huge difference in how I organized my life. It was so convenient! Of course, some of my students, who were 6 or 7 years of age at the time, had better smartphones than I did!

Nowadays, just like most people, I rely on my smartphone and the internet to keep me connected and help me run my online businesses. This technology has been a huge game-changer, and the internet has given me many opportunities that I would never have been able to get 20 years ago. In today's world, I can work from home (or anywhere for that matter). I've been able to build a business that can get clients and sales from anywhere in the world! In the old days, this never would have been possible.

That being said, there are some challenges to working online. For starters, I rarely work with other people. I spend a lot of time by myself in front of a screen, and I don't have a team or a company I work with. It can definitely become lonely at times. I started feeling like I never got away from my computer. I began to spend time outside of work checking work emails or communicating with clients. All of my time was basically being spent on one screen or another.

I slowly became more and more anxious, irritable, and miserable. My business was doing well, but this didn't mean much if I couldn't be happy. I knew that something had to change. If any of this sounds familiar to you, then you're probably not alone. Millions of people every year suffer from eye strain, neck stiffness, and general fatigue due to too much time spent on a phone or computer.

After taking some time to reflect on my situation, I

was eventually able to turn it all around. I still work online, but I have learned the necessary skills to be efficient with my screen time, and not spend too much of my life glued to my smartphone or computer. The time I spend now on social media is quite minimal, and my email box is no longer overflowing. I have a hard cut-off for work-related activities after 7:00 PM. I make it a priority to shut down and stop looking at my screen. I've also been taking a day off from my computer and smartphone once a week to do things like cooking, reading, visiting new places, etc. My life now is much more relaxed and happier, and I want to share this happiness with others who are in the same boat I was in years ago.

Now, I live as a writer, author, and marketer. I've published a number of bestselling books, and I've worked with clients earning more than 6 figures! I've travelled and lived in many various places, including Korea, Taiwan, Hong Kong, and Thailand, to name a few. My latest book, *The Art of De-cluttering,* is a bestselling title on Amazon, and now I want to expand my work to help people de-clutter their digital lives, as well.

Goals of this book

I'm writing this book to put together a set of exercises, and an actionable plan to help you reduce your reliance on technology. By taking the steps described in the following chapters, you will be able to balance your digital life and improve your mental health, reduce anxiety, and get more enjoyment out of life. I will also be showing you how to organize and de-clutter your computer, smartphone, and other devices so that you can get the most out of them without them consuming your life.

So, now the question becomes; *where do we start?* Well, let's start by going over the content of each chapter and what we will cover in each one:

Chapter 1: The Problems with Social Media and the Internet

Lots of people feel like the internet and social media are having a deep effect on our lives. However, many of us don't really think about how negative these effects can be. In this chapter, we'll be going over the original reasons that the internet and social media were introduced, and how their roles have evolved over time. We will also go over the negative effects that these things have begun to have on our day-to-day lives.

We'll be covering things like the negative impacts of social media, pornography addiction, and going over some of the studies that have been published regarding these issues. Then we'll go over practical examples of how these problems can take over our lives and make us depressed, or ineffective at completing tasks. On a lighter note, we'll also be going over some of the positive aspects of the internet and social media, and how we can use these things to make our relationship with technology healthier and more productive.

Chapter 2: Research and Studies

For this chapter, we'll be doing some in-depth analysis of the various science behind social media and internet addiction, and how these things affect us, as well as society at large. We'll be tying in some of the materials that we reviewed in chapter one in order to give a practical sense of how our digital lives affect our real lives and vice-versa.

Specifically, we'll be covering the scientific evidence for the various disorders caused by internet and social media addiction. These include, but are not limited to; depression, isolation, sleep problems, self-esteem problems, and many more. Learning how these things are caused by too much screen time is an important step toward identifying these digital influences in your day-to-day life.

Chapter 3: The Computer or Laptop

In this chapter, we'll dig into the nitty-gritty of desktop PC or laptop organization. I've been using computers to pursue my career pretty much from the beginning, and it has been a huge influence in my life for better or for worse. While computers definitely make our lives much more convenient, they can also make them a lot more stressful. For most of this chapter, we'll be going over practical step-by-step ways to get your PC organized.

We'll review best practices for things like file management and setting up a system for organizing all of your files. We'll also go through some exercises for getting rid of excess files we don't need, such as old photos or music we no longer listen to. We'll also review some more advanced solutions such as cloud storage, clearing your cache, and getting your registry in order.

Chapter 4: Emails

Organizing our email inbox can seem like an impossible task, especially if you are expected to correspond with colleagues for a certain amount of time every day. I personally have been using email since my high-school days, and recently I've been getting dozens of emails piling up in my inbox day after day. Most of these are emails from clients or otherwise related to my online business.

For this chapter, we'll go over some practical exercises for cleaning out our email inbox, organizing our subscriptions and newsletters and such. We will also learn to manage our email time so that it doesn't consume our lives. In particular, we'll be touching on the importance of organizing your email and work time so that you can effectively manage your inbox, without spending all day checking emails. We'll also outline best practices for handling your emails, as well as specific tips for Gmail versus Outlook.

Chapter 5: Social Media

Here we'll mostly be talking about the various effects that social media has on humans specifically. We'll expand on some of the things we talked about in chapter 1 and 2, and try to build some action plans for reforming our social media lives.

We'll be going over statistics from around the world on social media usage, as well as some of the most important scientific studies for understanding the effects that social media has on our mental health, as well as society. With this solid understanding of social media and how it affects our lives, we'll be able to identify problem areas and strategies for making sure we use social media responsibly.

We'll also go over proper social media management, and how to use apps and addons to get the most out of your social media experience, without having it drag you into compulsive behavior or stressed emotions.

Chapter 6: Time Management and

Productivity

For this chapter, we'll be reviewing everything we learned, and beginning to put it into practice as part of a coordinated effort to become more time-effective. The way we use digital solutions like the internet, smartphones, and social media can either make our lives more effective, or they can drag us down and make us less effective. Once we have learned the fundamentals of keeping our digital lives organized, we can see how these digital lives fit into a larger time-management scheme.

Specifically, we'll be learning how to keep focus, and divide our tasks so that we can tackle them efficiently and in a logical manner. We'll also go over ways to reduce workload and set effective goals for where we want to be in our lives. Along the way, we'll review how digital organization can help us manage our time, as well as how it can lead to us *losing* control.

We'll also go into detail about a few apps and programs you can use to help keep yourself organized in terms of time. Then, we'll give you some practical exercises for time management, and working digital de-cluttering into your regular routine. We'll also look at things like making lists of activities we can do rather than use social media.

Finally, we'll be going over the process of crafting your own 30-day plans for de-cluttering your devices, and handling your time management. So without further ado, let's get started de-cluttering our digital lives!

Chapter 1: The Problems with Social Media and the Internet

"Once a new technology rolls over you, if you're not part of the steamroller, you're part of the road."

-Stewart Brand

The internet started as a series of military intelligence networks in the 1970's called ARPANET. This eventually grew into the National Science Foundation Network. After lots of expansion through private networks, it eventually grew into the internet as we know it today around the early 1990's.

The initial purpose behind the internet and its precursors was to connect us. As it became bigger, and accessible to private citizens, it was supposed to make our lives easier. To a large extent, this is true. We no longer have to wait for snail mail to be delivered to talk to our friends far away; we can now receive information, educate ourselves, and even work for a living completely through the internet.

But there have been negative effects, as well. Pew Research Center has noted that *"There are circumstances under which the social use of digital technology increases awareness of stressful events in the lives of others.* This is especially true for women. What this means is that constantly being bombarded with turbulent information causes us to feel stressed. More and more people are also spending time isolated from their peers and other human beings. People are spending less and less time in person doing different things like they used to.

At the same time, there is less and less separation between work, online, and our personal lives. Every aspect of our lives is becoming merged together. After finishing a day of work, it is not uncommon for people to have to check their email to respond to bosses or clients.

What are the negative impacts of social media?

Social media is what keeps a lot of our world

connected these days. Even things like serious professional work are facilitated by social media sites such as *Linkedin*. While this has greatly accelerated the way in which we work and share information, it has also introduced a lot of negative influence to many people's lives:

- **Exposure to stressful information.** As we mentioned above, Pew research has found that constant exposure to things like depressing news headlines through social media increases the stress we feel day-to-day. A good example of this would be news about terrorist attacks, or natural disasters. Constantly hearing about the bad things happening in the world is bad for your psyche.

- **Self-esteem issues.** Forbes reports that social media can cause us to constantly compare our lives with the lives of others. This has the effect of making us feel inferior to those around us, causing self-esteem issues and widespread jealousy. This is a growing problem among children and young adults who use social media, since they are still developing and often spend a lot of time unsupervised on the internet.

- **Social media addiction.** Addiction Center notes that excessive social media usage can cause a kind of behavioral addiction. The dopamine rush that users get from receiving likes or being praised by their online "friends" causes a repeated habit of constantly turning to social media for validation. Many people experience some level of social media addiction throughout their lives, whether they are constantly obsessed with their likes and retweets, or simply checking their phone compulsively when they become stressed. Most people when they upload new posts, are expecting a dopamine rush. This can be disappointing if the likes and retweets are lower than expected. Eventually, this vicious cycle of posting and re-posting can make you feel like nobody cares about you, even though that probably isn't true.

- **Pornography Addiction.** This is one of the most insidious dangers of the internet. From a young age, children with smartphones have almost completely unsupervised access to pornography. This has led to widespread pornography addiction throughout the world. According to a study in *The APA Handbook of Sexuality and Psychology (vol. 2),* by Gert Martin Hald *et al.* between 50-99 percent of men regularly consume pornography. The rate is between 30 and 80 percent for women. Excessive pornography usage has been shown to lower testosterone and increase resistance to dopamine in the brain. This means that porn addicts must continue viewing more and more extreme pornography, leading to a vicious cycle of instant gratification. Another thing to keep in mind is that pornography is based on an idealization of reality, where we can experience any sexual gratification that we desire. If you don't find a particular video satisfying, you can simply click and see if the next one suits your fancy. However, real life is quite different from this experience. People are not perfect; they have flaws and needs. Relationships take time and effort to build, and you can't just click a mouse to get what you want.

These are only some of the negative aspects that the internet and social media have exacerbated in our day-to-day lives. We'll be looking at these effects and the research behind them in a later chapter, but for now, let's just take a moment to examine how social media and the internet affect *our* lives.

Everyone uses the internet differently, but it is very rare for somebody not to use it at all. Almost everybody uses the internet and social media to some degree, and it ultimately depends on your situation and lifestyle. If you run an online business, for example, you will be spending more time on the internet than your average person who just checks Facebook. You need to reply to emails, build sites, and many other things. Most people also use the internet as their primary mode of communication, so it's unrealistic to cut out the internet entirely.

However, the goal of this book is to give you the awareness and tools that you need to conquer addictions like this so that we can use the internet and social media to our advantage. Once you understand and remind yourself of the negative impacts social media and the internet are having on your life, you will find it much easier to let go and take the necessary steps to improve.

I understand that it will probably be hard for most people to disconnect, but it is possible, and the benefits can be tremendous. Once you get away from the damaging aspects of the internet and social media, you can really start to appreciate the benefits that it has for you. Some of these benefits include:

- **Open up social possibilities.** This is one of the most obvious effects, but many aspects of it are often overlooked. Social media allows people to connect with people in ways that were never possible before. This is especially true of individuals with impaired social skills, such as those with mental disabilities. Giving these people expanded social possibilities can directly increase their quality of life, as well as the opportunities available to them.

- **Inspire good life changes.** When you see your friends and others doing well on social media, sometimes it can drag you down and make you feel like everybody is making progress except for you. When we use the internet in a healthy way, however, it can also inspire us to improve our situation and take the necessary steps toward self-improvement.

- **Helping with medical research.** Social media sites are notorious for gathering, aggregating, and making use of customer data. One of the more positive aspects of this is that this data can be useful to mental health professionals who need to observe people's interactions in order to learn how the human mind can stay healthy. Social media also serves as a vector for volunteers who want to assist in studies or clinical trials.

- **Social support and interventions.** If you use social media responsibly, you can make a good mental health support system out of the people you know online. Of course, having friends and people you can count on in your real life are important too, but social media gives them a way to be connected to your life. It also gives people in crisis mode a way to reach out to others without harming themselves.

- **Opportunities to develop technical and other skills.** Using social media and the internet in general can give teens and young adults lots of opportunities to learn about tech, or any number of other fields. It is often very common for children who use social media to develop a kind of passive computer knowledge base. With some nurturing, this can become a marketable skill set such as programming or copy writing.

- **Living in the moment.** When you are no longer constantly absorbed in your phone or computer, you will be more conscious of the world around you. You will be able to notice and be thankful for things that are happening in the moment. You will recognize the value in the things you have in real life, and more able to take advantage of them.

- **Being open to real relationships.** Once you let go of your online "relationships" and "friends" that you only interact with through social media, you will become more open to forming relationships in real life. Human interaction without interruption from digital devices is more enjoyable, and helps form deeper interpersonal bonds than digital likes and retweets.

- **Reduced anxiety.** Taking control of your digital life will help you let go of your dependence on social media and the internet. If done properly, this will lead to you experiencing pleasant emotions more often, and having fewer anxious thoughts and emotions. You would be surprised how much simply checking your email compulsively can cause you stress.

These are only some of the benefits that a responsible digital life can bring you. When we learn how to organize our internet usage, digital device space, and social media time in later chapters, you will see how easy it can be to take control of your digital life.

Summary

- **Negative aspects of social media and the internet.** The internet and social media have introduced a large amount of negative influence in our day-to-day lives, and it can be easy to fall into self-destructive habits. Some of the more serious effects are suicidal thoughts or pornography addiction. Learning and understanding these effects can help us take control and understand why de-cluttering our digital life is so important.

- **Positive aspects of social media and the internet.** Although social media and the internet have a lot of negative effects, they are ultimately tools meant to help us succeed. When used responsibly, the internet can connect us in ways that were never possible before. We can even positively affect our mental and physical health by learning to live in harmony with the internet, rather than being dominated by it.

So that's about it for the first chapter. Hopefully, now you have a better understanding of what the internet is, and how social media affects our lives both positively and negatively.

In the next chapter, we'll be taking an in-depth look at some of the research behind what we covered in this chapter. We will also expand on some of the effects of internet and social media usage, and cover a few more things related to computer usage and best practices.

Chapter 2: Research and Studies

"If you're always trying to be normal, you will never know how amazing you can be."

-Maya Angelou

Like we touched on a bit in the first chapter, the digital age has introduced a large number of influences to our lives. Many of these influences are beneficial, but many of them also are not. It took researchers a long time to begin studying the effects of social media, since for many years, people did not take it seriously.

Nowadays, however, it is highly irregular for anybody not to have a social media account, and even more irregular for them not to use the internet at all. Even professional businesses these days perform many of their operations with the assistance of social media and the internet. Once researchers began looking at how human behavior had developed through exposure to the internet and social media, they began to see all kinds of complications.

For this chapter, we'll be going over as many of these negative effects as we can. We will examine the scientific evidence behind them in order to understand why they happen, and how we can help mitigate them. Since the internet and social media are very profitable and useful to many government agencies and businesses, it can be hard to find good research into the effects of using them. Many websites will flat-out lie to you and tell you that social media or pornography usage carries no risks whatsoever. Just like anything else in life, too much of *anything* can be bad for you. Even too much water or exercise can kill you!

For this reason, it is important to really examine the information presented to you, and make sure you understand the pitfalls that come with using social media and the internet, as well as computers in general. We will be using a large amount of studies from scientific journals and other reliable sources. Don't feel discouraged if you don't understand some of the more complex medical stuff, it's mostly meant to supplement your understanding of the risks.

The risks

While not an exhaustive list of every issue caused by social media and the internet, this list includes some of the most serious and most common effects that have been looked at by researchers and professionals:

- **Depression.** A study conducted in 2016 surveying 1700 people showed that people who used more social media platforms were three times as likely to suffer from depression. Another study from 2012 showed that negative emotions like feeling worthless were correlated with the quality of online interactions. What this means is that while social media doesn't directly cause depression, using it irresponsibly can have a negative impact on how we feel. Social media can cause depression in a number of ways. Among the most common are constant exposure to people who are "doing better"; constantly seeing tragic news in the media; and seeing other people receive more likes than you.

- **Isolation.** The American Journal of Preventative Medicine published a study in

2017 that showed 19-32 year-olds who spend the most time on social media were up to twice as likely to report feeling socially isolated. This includes a sense that they do not belong, a sense that engaging with others is difficult, and dissatisfaction with relationships. Feelings of isolation can be caused by problematic social media usage because artificial interactions replace face-to-face interactions, creating a dependence on artificial dopamine rushes rather than a healthy interpersonal relationship.

- **Sleep.** This is one of the most understood effects of digital device usage, as sleep research is a huge area of scientific study which often overlaps with research on social media and the internet. Researchers at the University of Pittsburgh in 2016 published a study where they examined the social media and sleep habits of 1700 18-30 year olds. What they found was that the largest factor in sleep disturbance from social media is the blue light from your screen. Blue light has been proven to have a toxic effect on the eye, as well as cause sleep disturbances. The researchers also found that the amount of times somebody logged on, rather than the amount of time they spent online, was largely correlated with sleep disturbance.

- **Addiction.** A study from 2012 showed that the popular social media website *Twitter* can be harder to quit than cigarettes or alcohol. While it's important to remember the seriousness of cigarettes and alcohol, it's also staggering to think that some people can have a harder time simply quitting social media. The reason for this is the feedback loop of positive stimuli that is created by many social media sites. Mobile games and other things like gambling use this trick as well, and it can be very dangerous for people who indulge too often.

- **Self-esteem.** This is one that many people know all too well. In 2016, researchers at Penn State University found that when people view other people's selfies too often, it can lower their self-esteem by making them feel they are inadequate by comparison. Researchers have also found that over half of users report feeling inadequate after using social media regularly. Debbie Bines, challenge events head for *Scope,* notes that "...when things get out of balance [with social media], we start comparing ourselves to others, or feeling irritated, jealous, or even ugly."

- **Happiness.** Although related to depression, this one is a bit different. Even if social media doesn't make you feel *depressed*, it can still impair your ability to feel happy. This idea is reinforced by a study from 2014 that shows people report low mood after using twitter compared to simply browsing the internet for the same amount of time. Researchers found that "...the longer people are active on Facebook, the more negative is*[sic]* their mood afterwards... this may be because people commit an affective forecasting error in that they expect to feel better after using Facebook, whereas, in fact, they feel worse."

- **Relationships.** Having an unhealthy relationship with your digital devices can hurt your real-life relationships as well. Another study from 2012 paired off groups of strangers, and tasked them with having a conversation with each other. One half of the groups had mobile phones on the table, while the other half had notebooks. The pairs that had mobile phones reported less meaningful interactions, and reported feeling less close to their conversational partner.

- **Envy.** This one can have a deep effect on our lives. The jealousy created by excessive social media usage can cause depression, make us feel inadequate, and put stress on our relationships. A study from 2018, for example, suggests that social media can cause jealousy in romantic relationships by exposing one partner to information about the other partner's romantic history. People in relationships often feel jealous when seeing their partner engage with people that they have had past relationships with, or getting attention from many people at once through social media.

- **Distraction.** We all know what it's like to spend too much time checking our phones or computers. It's just too easy with so much information at your fingertips. This can be particularly difficult with checking work emails when you should be doing something else, since it feels like you're doing something important. A study from the University of Waterloo in 2019 showed that 45% of undergraduate students reported using their cell-phones during class for reasons unrelated to the class itself.

- **Fear of missing out.** Fear of missing out is exactly what it sounds like. Being exposed to so much information at the same time in today's world can give us the chance to see incredible opportunities and events. Being constantly exposed to this information carries risks. The classic example is buying a new gadget that is being advertised because "Supplies are limited!" This kind of "FoMo" behavior is dangerous and can lead to bad decision making. A recent study showed that this type of trigger affects people of all ages on social media, not just children. In the study, which surveyed over 400 people across the United States, researchers noted that "we're not all equally prone to Fear of Missing Out, but for those who are, social media can exacerbate it."

- **Body image issues.** Constantly being exposed to images of celebrities can make us feel inadequate about our own bodies. This is especially true these days where people can post pretty much *anything* on social media. This problem also affects children and young adults very deeply, as they are still developing their idea of body image to begin with. Research shows a distinct connection between body image issues and social media usage (especially the viewing of images). Researchers found that brief exposure did not seem to negatively impact women's body image in general. However, social media usage does seem to negatively impact the body image of women who already have a tendency towards body negativity. (Holland & Tiggeman, 2016; Fardouly *et al.* 2014).

- **Other issues.** Social media causes a number of other problems. Because social media is largely passive consumption of information based on what you like and dislike, it can be easily manipulated by governments, publications, or even the platforms themselves. Case in point, analysis by Pew research center shows that roughly 20% of adults in the U.S. Get all of their news primarily from social media. This is a problem, since 90% of *all* media in the U.S. Only provides a singular uniform viewpoint on any given issue across multiple media. Pew research also suggests that adults who get their news primarily from social media also tend to believe in "conspiracies" more often than people who get their news from diverse sources.

These are only some of the most important problems that social media and internet misuse has been linked to. The purpose of this chapter is to educate you on the research behind these problems, and give you the tools to continue educating yourself on what is best for your brain and your life.

Resources

As we talked about earlier in the chapter, it can be difficult to find good information on this topic, since the vast majority of articles, shows, commentaries, and posts you see in media are heavily biased. Hope is not lost, though, because we still have some ways of getting good information, if you know where to look. Keeping yourself educated on the risks of digital clutter and social media abuse is one of the best ways to help you keep your devices as well as your life clutter-free.

- **Scientific journals.** The problem with articles is that they tend to summarize any actual science and make their own conclusions to suit whomever is paying for them to be made. If you actually take the time to read scientific publications behind the articles, you will be surprised to find that the conclusions are often completely different from the ones in the article you just read! Of course, scientific journals are not foolproof: many of them experience replicability crisis, and most of them are owned by the same company.

- **Statistics and data.** Plenty of agencies such as Pew Research Center perform surveys all the time to gauge how people are living in the world around them. If you educate yourself on the basics of statistical analysis (it's easier than it sounds), then you can easily use this information to educate yourself, rather than letting somebody else tell you what to think of it.

- **YouTube Channels.** YouTube can offer a nearly unlimited amount of video content. There are tons of educational channels for pretty much any topic. You can watch YouTube videos on history, politics, science, philosophy, and so much more. Just like anything else, it is important that you remember to watch a variety of different channels, so that you are exposed to more than one viewpoint. I myself used to get a lot of my news from one channel on YouTube. Eventually, I realized that this channel was fairly left-leaning, and they actually omitted a lot of facts and viewpoints for major issues. Only after I branched out did I end up learning more and being exposed to other viewpoints, realizing that they were only presenting one side of the story.

- **Audiobooks.** Audiobooks are a great way to consume written works. Especially if you don't have a lot of time to sit around reading actual books, audiobooks can be a huge boon. There are audiobooks available for most popular books or major classical works out there. You can even use software like ReadSpeaker to convert ebooks into audio format. This is really useful if you spend a lot of time commuting, or doing repetitive tasks where you could listen to an audiobook to learn while you work.

- **Further reading.** The most important thing to remember is that you have to do a *lot* of different reading and searching to get the information you need. If you get all of your information from a single source, or even a single *type* of source, chances are you are not seeing the full picture. The truth is, most types of media or content, no matter where they come from, are going to come with some type of bias. You have to come at it with an open mind.

So that's about it for the research side. Hopefully after reading this chapter, you have a better idea of the risks of social media, and how to keep yourself informed on the topic as it develops into the future.

Summary

- **Research shows that internet usage has its risks.** From depression to anxiety and everything in between. Understanding the relationship between online habits and mental health/organization is extremely important for using computers and social media effectively.

- **Knowing is half the battle.** Doing your own research and keeping the risks in mind while you re-organize your digital life will make it a lot easier to stay on track as you try to change your habits.

In the next chapter, we'll be digging into the nitty-gritty of organizing our computer files, desktops, and more!

Chapter 3: The Computer or Laptop

"The computer was born to solve problems that didn't exist before."

-Bill Gates

Computers are amazing machines. Since their inception, they have been used to crack codes that were thought impossible to break; they have made it easy and accessible to create and consume media; and they have brought a world full of people into a shared, connected space.

When I got my first computer, I couldn't believe how cool it was that I could scan documents and send them to my relatives halfway across the world instantaneously. The internet opened up a whole new world for me, and I currently live largely through this world due to my online businesses and correspondence.

Fast forward to today, and I am now using my computer on a daily basis in order to run my business.

I've been able to make it work, but keeping track of all the files and learning the make the most of the computer can be a challenge at times. When your files and habits are out of order, using the computer can become more of a time suck than it is a convenience.

In this chapter, we're going to go over some of the ways I've found work best for organizing your computer or laptop. Many of these principles will play a large role in organizing our other devices later on, as well. The key is to come up with a system and rehabilitate your bad habits.

Create a system for organizing your computer

If you don't have some kind of system in place for organizing your files, then there will be no rhyme or reason to how they are downloaded and stored in your computer. Chances are that this will get out of hand very quickly; *especially* if you do a lot of work over the computer such as freelance or online marketing.

There are dozens of ways of organizing your files, which range from simple to quite complex. It might seem like an impossible task to organize your files, but once you take a look and start making an effort, it often becomes much easier than it looks.

Here are some of the basic organization systems that many people use to arrange their files on their computer. Different approaches work better for different types of people and different types of online work, so think hard about until your needs and find a method that suits them.

- **Project-based System.** For this structure, every file that you work with is arranged and organized according to the different projects you are working on, and possibly also by client if you work with multiple people at once. This means creating folders for each project (or client), and keeping all of the files for that project/client in the same, clearly marked folder. This has the advantage of putting everything you need for a single project in one place. It can be especially useful for people with online businesses or who do freelance work for multiple clients. If you don't work on multiple projects, or if your computer work is more personal/creative, this might not be the method for you. Keep in mind that organizing files *within* each project folder is still important. It's a good idea to merge this system with some of the others in order to keep project files within the same folder organized.

- **Date-Based System.** This one is pretty straightforward. Date based file management systems use the date that files were created or modified as a reference point for organizing them. You can create folders for the years and months in which you work, and keep the files you created or worked with for that period organized in the corresponding folder. This system is convenient if you need to do a lot of referencing of old work, or if you have trouble finding old files when they are needed again. This structure tends to work best for people who perform repeated weekly or monthly tasks on their computer. Especially if you regularly receive new reports or files that have similar names with a few numbers changed, this method can help you keep them organized without getting a headache. The problems with a date-based system is that it can be a little bit much to manage. If you aren't receiving or modifying multitudes of documents of varying time periods, then keeping different folders for each month can be kind of overkill. Another important thing to consider is *which date* to use for your reference point. It could be the date when the file was created, the date when it was last modified, or even the deadline for submission.

- **File-based system.** For this system, we use the different file *types* that we work with in order to organize our files. This method is not related exclusively to computer file types, either. You can organize your files in folders like "Images" or "Statements", rather than having a different folder for *every* single file type. This typically works best for organizing files within a larger system, such as the project-based system. When you try to use this as your main structure, it can quickly become confusing to keep track of many files at the same time. Consider applying a file-based system within one of your project or date-based folders if you are experiencing difficulty coordinating files within those folders.

These are the three basic systems for organizing files on your computer. Generally speaking, you will be using a combination of all three depending on the type of work you do on your computer. Many more complex systems for file organization are based on the principles of these three systems.

The important thing is to play around with the different systems and find the one that works for you. Keeping your work organizes isn't about following instructions down to the letter; you have to experiment and work out the methods that work best with your activities.

Organizing your desktop

The desktop is one of the most important aspects of your file system. This is the dashboard from which the rest of the work that you do will begin. Some people like to keep very minimal desktops, while others end up with huge messes of files and folders with no real rhyme or reason.

Not only does organizing your desktop give you easy and organized access to some of your most used files and programs, but it also creates a clear and aesthetically pleasing dashboard for you to work with. This kind of de-cluttering is important for its psychological impact as well as its practical purpose.

So how do we go about organizing the desktop? Just like anything else, there are a number of ways to do this, and the one you use will depend on a number of factors. How often do you actually *use* your desktop? Do you find yourself looking around your desktop frequently trying to find files? Do you often install programs that drop shortcuts on your desktop by default?

The answers to all these questions will make a difference in how you organize your desktop. There are a few basic principles we can follow to get started:

- **Sort by.** Windows computers actually have a function that allows you to automatically sort the files on your desktop. Simply right-click the desktop and mouse over the "Sort by" option. Here, you will be given the choice of organizing your icons by name, size, type, or date. While this function is a nifty little tool that can help you keep your desktop organized, it is still important to manage the files on your desktop and make sure you are using the space effectively.

- **Use the start menu and taskbar.** Having all of your icons on your desktop can *seem* convenient, but it definitely is not if you have to spend ten minutes squinting every time you want to find an important file or program. If you use the space on your taskbar or start menu to hold some of your more commonly used shortcuts, it will free up a lot of space on your desktop for other files and icons.

- **Use folders to organize files.** Just like with general file management, organizing your desktop can be helped quite a bit by using folders to organize your shortcuts. This is especially useful if the icons on your desktop can easily be separated into a few different categories, or if you use your desktop as a temporary work space. Consider organizing your desktop by type, date, or project, just like with general file management.

- **Use apps or widgets to help you organize your files.** If you still have trouble organizing your desktop, or you just want things to look more organized with info at a glance, it might be a good idea to use some apps or widgets to help you organize your desktop. There are plenty of options available for dividing your desktop into sections, or grouping icons with pertinent information displayed alongside them. Something like Stardock Fences is a good place to start.

  https://www.stardock.com/products/fences/

- **Use naming conventions.** This is a great piece of advice for organizing your computer in general, so it's a good idea to wrap your head around it now so you can get used to it. Make sure that when you name files, the way that you name them is informative, concise, and accessible. If you give all of your files random names, it will be impossible to organize them properly! Common things to include in a name would be the title, date, your name or the client's name, and any other pieces of information you will want to know without opening the file every single time. Try and avoid long names, if you can, since if the file name trails off into an ellipsis, you won't be able to read it, and your efforts will have been in vain.

- **Tidy your desktop regularly.** This is one of the most important habits to get into for keeping your desktop (and your computer in general) organized. If you only organize your files once, they probably will not stay organized. You want to be making an effort to clean regularly enough that you stay on top of the clutter, but not so often that it takes too much time out of your schedule. It's a good idea to always do this on the same day of the week (or month), so that you build the habit of performing a cleanup regularly. How often you do this will depend on how often your computer and desktop require cleaning up. If you work on a lot of different projects, or with many different file types that are constantly clogging up your desktop, it's a good idea to organize your files more often. If you don't often deal with a large volume of files, it is much easier to do it as needed, or just less frequently.

Keeping your desktop organized could fill an entire chapter by itself, but these are the basic best-practices for keeping your desktop free of clutter. If you want more information, or suggestions for more software for helping to keep your desktop organized, there is plenty of information available online for you. Doing your own research and experimentation is one of the best ways to find apps and solutions that work for you.

Organizing your photos

This one can be tricky for some people, because many photos and pictures can have sentimental value that makes us want to hold on to them. The problem with this is that we often wind up with hundreds or even *thousands* of images clogging up our computers. For many people, they will rarely actually look at the pictures that they keep on their computer, making them completely pointless clutter.

The main way to avoid this is to simply delete photos that you never view. Go through your picture folder(s) and check each photo. Ask yourself "do I ever look at this photo?" and "is this photo *useful* to me in some way?" If the answers are no, *delete the picture.* There's no point in holding on to a photo and letting it take up space if you never look at it. If the photos are important (for example, deceased loved ones), then consider having them printed or keeping them on a dedicated external hard drive. When deleting photos to free up space*; be ruthless.* You will never be able to organize your photos if you can't let go of the ones you don't need.

Now, of course, if you're a graphic designer, or somebody who uses a lot of photos for their work or hobby, this will be more of a daunting task. If you use photos and images in a professional context, then you should definitely have a naming convention and folder system in place to help you track which pictures belong to each project on which you are working.

So, now that we've tackled some of the extra photos that we don't need, we can go over some ways to help us organize the ones that we keep:

- **Create a digital photo hub.** If you work with a lot of photos professionally, or if you have a large number of photos that you just can't get rid of (I told you to be ruthless!), it's a good idea to set up a digital photo hub. Think of this as the place where you choose to organize all of your photos. This can be a separate device from your main computer, a specific location on your computer, or even some sort of cloud storage solution.

- **Choose a system for organizing your photos.** Just like with your files in general, having a system in place for organizing your photos is essential. You *could* just use the same date/type/project systems that we went over earlier, but sometimes images can be a bit tricky. Some projects use different types of photos for different things. For example; banners, logos, and backgrounds for an internet website. In these cases, it is best to use sub-folders to keep everything nice and clean. If you're a web designer, you might have a few different image-based templates that you need to organize by color or style, which adds to the complexity of keeping your image folder organized. Think about all the different images you have, and what they're used for. Experiment with different systems and try to find one that suits your needs.

- **Manage your output folders.** This one is very often overlooked. Whenever you save an image from the internet, import a picture from your camera, or save a new image you were working on in Photoshop, that image is sent somewhere on your computer. If you don't use the *Save As* option, these files usually get dropped into some kind of default location. Different programs will typically use different default locations for their image files, which can make you end up with different images all over your computer. This is no good. Go through all the different programs you use to interact with images (don't forget your internet browser!), and set the default output folders so that they make sense. Generally, it is good to have them all output to a similar location, but not the *same* location. Since you use different programs for different things related to images, having them all output to the same folder would mix them all up. Instead, try to integrate your output settings so that they make sense with your image organization system. For example: if you're a copy writer who often needs to use stock images in their work, you will want to set your internet browser to download images to the folder where you keep resources for your projects.

- **Organize photos according to attributes.** This can be especially useful if you are a photographer who stores many different photos. Try organizing your photos based on the color, orientation, type of shot, or subject. This will make it easier to find photos that suit your needs from among your droves of image files. For example, if you need a photo that looks good in a room with blue walls, you will want a picture with predominantly blue tones. If you have your photos arranged by dominant color, this will be an easy thing to do. If you don't have a large number of photos, or if you don't actually use the photos for projects or hobbies, then this might be wasted effort. Still; consider how you use your images and think about whether or not organizing them by their attributes would make your life easier.

- **Keep backups.** This is especially important *during* the process of re-organizing your images, so that you don't accidentally delete an image that you wanted to keep. Backing up your images in general helps you feel confident deleting ones you don't need on your computer. The one thing that is important to keep in mind is that a good backup needs to be accessible and secure. There is no sense locking all your backups away on a hard drive that you don't have access to. Likewise, you won't want to keep photos with sensitive content in a place where they could be accessed by other people. Cloud storage can be a good solution for backing up your files, but having some kind of hard solution is also a good idea. Google Drive is an excellent resource for cloud storage solutions, allowing you plenty of room and features, even with a free account. *Dropbox* is another good option. If you want something more, *IDrive* provides 5 Terabytes of storage for $3.98. For external hard drives, Amazon has plenty of good options; such as the *Silicon Power Armor A60*.

- **Differentiate between personal photos and business photos.** If you use photos in your work or hobbies, make sure to store them separately from your personal photos, so that they don't get mixed up. This is another area where cloud storage is your friend. If you have a large number of personal photos taking up room in your storage, consider deleting some of them (refer to earlier in the chapter and remember to *be ruthless)*.

Organize your video files

Video files are a lot like images. The difference is that they are typically much larger in file size, and can be a pain to move around or store as a result. The trade-off is that we generally have fewer videos on our computers than we have images. The exception to this is if you use video files for work, like if you're a video editor or work in video marketing.

It's also less simple to get information at-a-glance from a video thumbnail. With images, you can see exactly what the image is from the thumbnail (except for small details). With videos, the thumbnail could be something completely unrelated to the video itself. This makes it all the more important to organize and properly name your video files when storing them.

Another problem with video files is the various formats in which they are stored. With images, you can generally be sure that different file types generally behave the same way when opened or used with various programs. With video files, this becomes more complex. People these days often take videos with a number of different devices, and this can have a profound effect on how we organize them. That being said, there are still a number of basic principles we can follow to help organize our video files:

- **Manage videos on your device.** Chances are that most of you reading this are taking videos primarily with your smartphone or other mobile device. If you shoot video with your phone frequently, you might even have a large bank of random videos stored up in your phone with little rhyme or reason. It doesn't make sense to upload or sync all of these random videos on your computer without trimming the fat a bit first. Regularly go through the videos on your phone and delete ones that you haven't watched in a while, or ones with similar content that you have already shot before. You can also eliminate things like viral videos, which can be seen elsewhere without taking up space on your computer.

- **Store videos in a central location.** Just like with pictures, video files can end up all over your computer in various file types, and this can be a nightmare for organization. Storing your videos in a common place on your hard drive helps you keep everything organized without jumping back and forth all over your hard-drive. Employing an organization system for keeping this central hub under control is also essential, just like for image files and files in general. If you work with videos a lot, then organizing them by project is probably your best bet. If you download a lot of random videos, or if you store a lot of videos of important events in your life, a date-based system will probably work better.

- **Keep backups.** Just like with image files, keeping regular backups of your video library will help you trim and organize your video collection without worrying that you will lose something important. Since video files are much larger than images or documents, it can be a pain to store them on your hard drive. Cloud services such as iCloud for iPhone users, or Google Drive for android users are good options for storing your backups.

- **Keep it simple.** If you feel like there are way too many videos to sort, or you don't know the best way to sort them all, a good rule of thumb is to *keep it simple*. Trying to figure out a complex system for tracing your video files can be time consuming and confusing. This is especially true when a simple date or project-based system would suffice. If you prefer, you can start with a simple system for the initial sorting, and choose a more specialized system after you've gotten a handle on what you're doing.

- **Track your shoots.** If you do a lot of filming, and end up with large amounts of videos on your devices, then you might want to keep a simple record of when, where, and why you shot each video. This will give you a concrete reference point for why each video exists and where it came from. A simple excel spreadsheet would suffice. This is especially useful for students in film-related courses or people who work with videos for a living.

Organizing your music

Since the advent of the internet, the world of music has absolutely exploded. Today, you can hear death metal from Indonesia, or rap from the Arctic Circle if you wanted to. What this means is that many people now have much larger libraries of music that they want to listen to. This can make it tricky to keep track of all your music.

Another problem is that in order to listen to music the way you want, it has to be organized in a way that is accessible and provides for your listening needs. Most people don't just want individual songs, but also playlists or even recommendations for music they haven't heard before.

Obviously, if you simply keep all your music in a huge folder and use the search function to find the songs you want, this is hardly an effective strategy for managing your music. There is a lot of different music playing software out there, and a lot of it is quite comprehensive for typical listening needs. The problem is that storing music on your computer can quickly become less than economical if you have a library with several thousand hours worth of tracks. This problem gets worse if you want to keep your songs in an archival format such as FLAC.

One of the best solutions to these problems is to use a music streaming service such as Spotify or Apple Music. These apps allow you to stream music to your device without actually downloading and storing it on your computer. They also have other features like being able to make playlists and receive music recommendations, making them a great solution for storing your music.

If you work with audio files for work or your hobbies, this is less of an option. You will still need to follow some best practices in order to keep your files organized and allow for efficient work. For this, we can follow a few simple steps:

- **Use descriptive file names.** It can be impossible to work with a library of music if everything is labelled with random names, numbers, and other information. Pick a naming convention for your audio files and stick to it. For audio files, good things to include in the file name are a title related to the content, maybe some descriptive tags, and also perhaps the codec that the video was encoded with. If you aren't an editor or hobbyist, don't worry too much about the codec, stick with whatever information keeps the file names practical for your usage.

- **Update the metatags.** If you've done any

reading on the topic of audio files, or computer storage in general, you have probably heard the phrase "metadata" somewhere at some point. Basically, metadata is hidden data which your computer uses to identify things about your files. Metadata is used to categorize different pieces of information such as artist, title, date of release, and other information. Keeping this information up-to-date for your audio files can really help you keep track of them. If your music metadata is properly configured, then programs like Windows Media Player will be able to automatically identify the music without you having to manually remember or guess what it is. In order to edit metadata, you will need specialized software. Here is a guide on how to manage your metadata.

http://bit.ly/metadata-guide

- **Make sure to get music from *legal* sources.** This is kind of a no-brainer, but some people might not realize that pirating music has its disadvantages. When you download music illegally, it often comes with no meta information, and can end up in some random corner of your hard drive, taking up space. Obtaining music only from legal sources, such as iTunes, means that your library will be up-to-date with all of the necessary metadata, and it will also remain located in a consistent output folder on your computer.

How to keep your programs organized

If you've been following all the tips so far, and taking the time to really sift through your files and make sure everything is in order, then your computer is probably starting to look a lot more organized. There is still plenty left to be done, though. After organizing our files, we should be taking a look at the various programs, plugins, and extensions we have installed on our computer.

Most people buy pre-built computers that come with a suite of software pre-installed. Many of these default programs are useful, but some are not and others can even be harmful. On top of this, many people download new programs for every little task and then don't take the time to delete them afterwards. There are few things more crippling for a PC build than being bogged down with unnecessary programs.

Go through the list of programs installed on your computer, and uninstall any of the ones you haven't used in a few months. If you have any programs set to run at Startup, even though you don't use them, uninstall these as well (or at least set them to not run at Startup). A great program for this is *Iobit Uninstaller*; it can identify large programs, programs that you don't use, or plugins/extensions that can be removed from your browser and other apps.

Cloud storage and backing up

We talked a bit about cloud storage and backups earlier, but here we can go a bit more in-depth into the best practices for using cloud storage and backups. Much like with your computer in general, your backups need to be organized and accessible, otherwise there is no point in keeping them in the first place.

The first thing to remember is that folders are your friend. Pick a system for organizing, and separate your files into different folders based on the system you choose. For backups, date-based systems tend to work well because you will often be storing files that you don't use or that you downloaded a long time ago. Of course, you will want to go through your files regularly to make sure that you aren't holding on to anything unnecessary.

In terms of which cloud services to use, here are some of the most popular ones:

- **Google Drive.** This is probably the most popular solution out there, as it can be easily integrated with other tools such as Google Docs. The free account gives you up to 15GB of storage space, with upgrades available up to 200GB for around 4 dollars a month.

- **Dropbox.** Another solid option; Dropbox is a simple and effective cloud storage solution that has apps available for just about every device and OS on the market. It supports collaboration between users and has an excellent feature set for the *Pro* option. The free version, however, is rather limited at 2GB.

- **Onedrive.** This is Microsoft's cloud storage

solution. This one is nicely integrated with Windows 10 and Office 365, as can be expected from a Microsoft product. It also features collaborative editing. The free storage option is a bit better than Dropbox at 5GB.

- **IDrive.** This is a nice lesser-known option with easy setup and some cool features. Where IDrive really shines, however, is their premium packages. Premium users with IDrive can get up to 5 Terabytes of space for around 4 dollars.

Optimizing your computer

Files and programs are not the only things that take up space on our computers. There are caches and temporary files and loads of different things that will slow down our OS and make it frustrating to organize the rest of our stuff.

Thankfully, you don't need to be super tech-savvy to keep these things clean. There are lots of programs and apps to help us along the way, which we will review in a moment. First, we'll go over some of the best practices for optimizing our devices. Keep in mind that many of these things also apply to mobile devices!

- **Keep device drivers up to date.** Your graphics card, and other devices on your computer such as microphones and speakers, use programs called *drivers* in order to function. Keeping these up to date ensures that these devices always work properly.

- **Keep your OS up to date.** Just like with your device drivers, your Operating System receives regular updates that keep it running as efficiently as possible. Making sure that your OS is up to date avoids issues of compatibility with new software or updates from the developer.

- **Keep your antivirus up to date.** This one is really important. You need some kind of software in place for scanning and removing viruses. Keeping these up to date means that they will always be aware of new viruses and other threats, as well as being able to take care of them when they infect your computer.

Now that we have that out of the way, let's go over

some of the things we need to keep our computer optimized:

- **Clearing caches.** Many programs keep caches of files for configuration and other purposes. These files tend to build up and can quickly bog down things like your internet browser, as well as your computer in general. Use a program like CCleaner *Advanced System Care* to clean your cache regularly.

- **Cleaning registry entries.** Your computer keeps a "registry" of all the different programs and files in order to keep track of them for internal operations. If left unchecked, this registry can become convoluted with double entries, or old entries that are no longer necessary. CCleaner and *Advanced System Care* are great options, as well.

- **Clearing histories and temporary files.** Programs such as internet browsers keep histories and lots of temporary files that are mostly unnecessary once they build up over time. Cleaning them regularly is important to keeping your programs running smoothly.

Advanced System Care is also great for this
one.

- **Disk defragmentation.** Your hard disk
actually stores information as a physical
etching onto the disk. However, sometimes,
due to space restrictions, a single file may need
to be stored as "fragments" in two different
physical spaces on the disk. This causes the
reader to jump back and forth between points
on the disk in order to read different parts of
the same file, which slows down your
computer. In order to combat this, you must
regularly defragment your drives with a
program like *Smart Defrag.*

- **Virus scans.** Viruses, malware, spyware, and
all kinds of other fun goodies are floating
around the internet just waiting to take
advantages of vulnerabilities in your system. A
good firewall can stop most of them, but it's
impossible to stop *every* single virus from
getting through, especially if you download a
lot of files for your job or hobby. To avoid
damage to your system, you should regularly be

scanning for and eliminating malware with some sort of anti-malware program. Some of the most popular options for this are *Avast Antivirus, Malwarebytes Anti-Malware,* and *IoBit Malware Fighter.* If you have a pre-built PC or laptop, it's very likely that your computer came with some form of antivirus pre-installed.

Aside from optimizing your computer with the above methods, it is also important to manage your time when using the computer to avoid wasting time. Using a timer to break up tasks with small breaks in between often works best. We will be going over time management in a later chapter, but it deserves a mention here, nonetheless. I personally use a program called *Take a Break* to manage my breaks.

Keeping internet browsers organized

Internet browsers are the primary way that we interact with the world wide web. However, they often incorporate a lot of extra software extensions, temporary data, and other stuff that we don't really need. You can also end up cluttering your computer based on the sites that you visit, or which sites are allowed to open notifications and access parts of your computer. It's important to keep these things in check if we want to keep our digital lives organized.

- **Check apps and extensions.** Go into your Google Chrome, Firefox, Safari, or whatever browser you use and check the installed plugins, extensions, and apps. Make sure that you only have the ones that you need or want installed. Try and eliminate as many of these as possible.

    ○ To check your extensions in Google Chrome, click on the three dots in the top right-hand corner of the window (the menu button), and click on "more tools" > "extensions". This will bring u a list where you can manage your extensions and grab new ones. You can also simply type *chrome://extensions* into the URL bar.

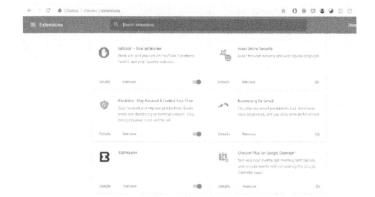

- To check your extensions in Safari, click on "Safari" > "Preferences", and then navigate to the "Extensions" tab. Here you can see a list of installed extensions and disable the ones you don't need.

- **Manage cookies and notifications.** Cookies are data that is sent to your computer from websites, which is sent back by your computer after being stored. They allow sites to track usage data and things like usernames or passwords. Generally, you will want to avoid using cookies so that websites don't track the things that you do. These can be disabled or enabled in your browser settings, as well as cleared by clearing your history.

○ To manage cookies in Google Chrome, click on the three dots in the top-right corner of the Chrome window, and then click "Settings". Navigate to the "Privacy and Security" > "Cookies and other site data". Here you can choose to allow block cookies, and even manage cookies for specific websites.

Clear browsing data

Basic	Advanced

Time range   All time   ▼

☐ Browsing history
Clears history from all signed-in devices. Your Google Account may have other forms of browsing history at myactivity.google.com.

☑ Cookies and other site data .
Signs you out of most sites. You'll stay signed in to your Google Account so your synced data can be cleared.

☐ Cached images and files
Frees up 319 MB. Some sites may load more slowly on your next visit.

Cancel   **Clear data**

To manage cookies in Safari, click on "Safari" > "Preferences" > "Privacy" > "Manage Website Data." This will display a list of all the websites that have stored cookies on your computer. You can choose to delete specific cookies from the list, or clear your cookies entirely.

- **Manage website access.** Restricting which sites your browser can access will help manage the amount of threats and unnecessary data your system is exposed to. Block sites like pornography sites or sites that waste your time without helping you in any way. There are also browser extensions, such as *Blocksite*, that will help you do this.

- **Only use the internet for research and work.** Stay away from excess internet time outside of research and work. If you do use the internet outside of work, try to limit your usage with a timer to keep yourself productive and mentally healthy. Personally, I only use social media after completing my work around 7PM. I also limit myself to around 20 minutes per day. I use a Chrome extension called *Waste No Time* to help accomplish this.

- **Consider taking time off from the internet.** Taking time away from your devices for one day each week can have profound effects on your productivity and outlook.

Diversifying the way you spend your time, such as getting out and trying new things, has proven to be healthier than sitting in the same room every day doing the same things. Pick a day out of your week where you are less busy and try doing a new activity to keep you busy on that day.

Staying focused

Becoming distracted from your work kills your productivity. Many of us don't realize just how many distractions we deal with in our offices or homes. Keeping these distractions to a minimum will help you stay on task, but it's also a good idea to establish habits that encourage productivity and decrease distraction.

- **Take breaks.** This may seem counter-intuitive, but taking regular breaks from your work can actually help your productivity. Taking breaks helps break up the monotony of your work, and can stop you from getting burned out and grinding to a halt. I use an app called *Scirocco* to help me schedule my break time.

- **Take breaks away from the computer.** Doing something that isn't computer-related in between your work periods can help keep your juices flowing and your brain happy. Try doing stretches or reading a book in between rather than browsing Facebook or Twitter. Studies have shown that too much sitting is bad for your health, so force yourself to get up and walk around once every hour.

- **Log Off.** Your devices will continue sending notifications and trying to suck you back onto your computer if you let them. Log off of all your social media accounts and devices to avoid this and increase productivity. Remember to turn off your phone, or at least set it to silent mode. Better yet, put the phone away in a drawer or somewhere else where you won't be tempted to check it. This will train your brain to not instantly react to notifications. No message or notification is so important that it cannot wait a couple of hours for a response. If it was that urgent, they would tell you. Personally, I schedule my email checks and responses twice a day, at 12PM and 6PM. That's it.

- **Use apps to help you stay focused.** Aside from time management apps to help you manage your work schedule, there are also some extensions you can use to help keep you from getting distracted online. A good option is an extension for Google Chrome called *StayFocused*. This app actually lets you set time limits for certain websites, and will kick you off if you spend too long on them. *Waste No Time* is another option that I personally use. You can also turn off your wifi during work, or enable "Focused Mode" on your phone, which allows you to only access certain apps.

Summary

We've learned a lot in this chapter, so let's go over some of the main takeaways that you should keep in mind when going forward and trying to keep your computer or laptop organized:

- **Create a system.** In order to organize our files, we need to decide on how to organize them. Use folders to split your files into different categories (organized by date, file-type, or project). Stick to your system for keeping files organized; manage the output folders of the various programs you use to keep new files organized.

- **Organize your desktop.** Delete unwanted icons and files. Use shortcuts on your taskbar or start menu rather than just your desktop in order to save space. Consider separating your desktop into different sections, or using your desktop as a temporary workspace.

- **Delete unneeded photos.** Ask yourself if you ever really look at pictures, and what you get out of keeping them. Organize photos based on tags like color and subject. If you're a photographer or professional designer, organize your photos according to project or shoot. Use cloud storage or an external hard drive to keep backups of your photo collection.

- **Back up your photos.** Keeping backups of your files helps you feel confident deleting the ones that are taking up space on your computer, as well as giving you an easily organized way of accessing your backed-up files. Remember to keep your cloud storage or external hard drive organized with appropriate folders and file systems (sorting by date is recommended for backups, specifically).

- **Keep video files organized.** Make sure your videos are named accurately in order to keep track of them. Organize them according to content or by project. If you're a photographer, organizing your videos according to when and where they were shot is also a good idea. Use cloud storage or external hard drives to store all your videos in a central location for easy access. Cloud storage is good for backing up your files to avoid losing them.

- **Organize your music library.** Use descriptive file names for all of your music files to keep them well-organized and accessible at a glance. Update and verify the metatags for your music files so that programs such as iTunes or Windows Media Player can identify details about them and keep them properly organized. Make sure to get music only from legal services to avoid missing metadata or viruses, as well as to help your music player keep them organized. Consider using a streaming app such as Spotify or even YouTube to listen to your music rather than keeping all of it on your computer itself.

- **Use cloud storage or external hard drives for backups.** Keeping backups of all your files on the same device doesn't make a lot of sense, does it? Use a cloud storage solution like Google Drive, Dropbox, Onedrive, or IDrive in order to keep your backups and other files organized on a separate system. Cloud computing works great for backups because the data can be retrieved even if all of your devices fail.

- **Optimize your computer.** Computers store a lot of extraneous information in the form of registry entries, cached data, temporary files, and much more. Understanding these different components and how to stay on top of them is essential for keeping your computer optimized and running smoothly. Using software like Advanced System Care or other IoBit solutions can help you clear your cache, delete unnecessary files, and keep your registry free of errors and bad data.

- **Optimize your internet usage.** Manage your internet usage so that you stay productive and avoid wasting your time. There are many websites out there designed to distract you and keep you from doing important stuff, so keeping this under control is essential for productivity. Use apps to manage your internet time or even block sites that you know will serve as a distraction for you.

- **Stay focused.** Learn to take regular breaks in order to stay productive and avoid burnout.

Take your various breaks away from your computer and other devices to break up the monotony and keep the juices flowing. Log off of your social media and various devices to avoid sliding back into the habit of checking Facebook or twitter. Consider setting aside one day a week where you don't use digital devices or the internet. Use the internet only for research and work. Do something else during your breaks, such as reading a book or studying a language.

In the next chapter, we'll be taking a look at our email inbox, and how to get it organized.

Chapter 4: Email

"Email is a system that delivers other people's priorities to your attention. It's up to you to decide when that priority should be managed into your world. It's not the other way around."

-Chris Brogan

The first time I began using email was in high school. It was quite an exciting time, singing up for Hotmail so that I could communicate with my friends. Nowadays, I get dozens of new emails every day. Not just important emails from clients but also junk mail, random subscriptions, and all kinds of other stuff.

If I left my inbox alone even for a little bit, it would quickly grow out of control. I was spending so much time answering emails that I knew I needed to make a change. That's when I did what most people have a hard time imagining; I deleted everything and started fresh. I unsubscribed from every newsletter I was receiving, and started only checking my email at specific times of the day.

Email overview

Many people receive tons of email in a day. Radicati reports that the average American worker receives a whopping 126 emails every single day! That's over 41 *billion* emails being received across the US on any given day. Out of these emails, a huge number of them are junk emails, unsolicited marketing campaigns and advertisements, political pandering, and more.

With such a volume of communication coming and going from our inbox each day, it's no wonder that many people find it hard to stay on top of their email pile. Statista reports that up to 82% of workers admit to checking their work email outside of normal business hours.

If we spend too much time checking emails, not only does it take up the time we spend outside of work. But it can make us feel like we never actually stop working. Learning to let go and limit the amount of time you spend answering emails is an essential step of de-cluttering your digital life.

Tips for email management

The key to checking email without it taking over your

life is to limit the time you spend checking emails. You should be able to limit your email time to two manageable chunks of your day, preferably one at the beginning and one at the end.

Gary Keller wrote a phenomenal book on successful habits that he calls *The One Thing*. He found the most success in managing his life when he learned to focus on the task at hand. When he did not succeed, he found that it was because his priorities were too spread out and unfocused. We need to bring this level of focus to our email management:

- **Limit yourself to checking email twice a day.** Set times at the beginning and end of the day to check emails. Make it so that you won't be distracted by other things during this period. The point is to get yourself to focus on the emails so that you can manage them and move on to more important things.

- **Learn to write emails effectively and concisely.** One of the best ways to reduce back-and-forth with clients and other contacts is to make sure that your emails are concise and effective. Proper composition is practically an art form, but there are a few simple rules you can follow to keep your emails short and sweet:

1. Develop an "email voice" Don't type the way you speak, but don't make it too formal either. It should sound natural without any extra words.

2. Write out what you want to say, but try to stay on topic. Don't stuff too many subjects into your email. Try to limit yourself to three sentences for each paragraph, and then move on.

3. Edit your message; remove duplicate information; try to eliminate extra words (e.g. *In order to* rather than simply *to*)

4. Think about the point of your email as a single sentence, or 2-3 if necessary. Now read over your email. Did you get your point across? Is it easy to understand? Is there anything that is irrelevant to the purpose of the email?

5. Rinse & repeat until you feel comfortable. You shouldn't have to take more than a few minutes to type and send an email. Try setting a timer for yourself for 5 minutes next time you have to write an email.

6. For example: I've received an email from a client who needs help with his blog or website content. My email would read something like this:

I would be happy to help you with your blog content.

How did you hear about my services?

How many blog posts do you need?

How many words do you need per blog post?

Do you have a specific budget in mind?

You can learn more about my services here:

Please let me know if you have any questions.

Kind regards,

Alex

- ○ First of all, the email is professional and friendly. I ask them where they heard about my services (this can be valuable information for marketing yourself), and then I ask them about the details of the job so that I can give them an accurate quote. I also asked about the budget to see whether or not it's feasible for us to work together to meet the client's needs.

- ○ Lastly, I encourage them to follow up by asking them to let me know if they have any questions. In marketing, this is called a "call to action", or CTA.

- Use *Grammarly.* Grammarly is a great tool that you can install as an extension to automatically check your grammar, vocabulary, spelling, and more. I regularly use it for all of my emails and working in Google Chrome.

- **Use Boomerang.** This is another useful tool that allows you to automatically send emails, track responses and use AI to guide your email composition.

- **Sort your emails.** Most email clients will already automatically sort many of your emails into different sections, but adding more of your own can help cut down on the clutter. Think back to the file management systems that we talked about in chapter 3. Consider using date-based or client-based systems for organizing your emails. Some of the folders I personally use include my ads, clients, email marketing, and more.

- **Spend time tweaking your spam filter.** The spam filter is your best friend when it comes to checking your email. Making sure that it is properly configured to stop the mail that you don't want to see is essential. If you're receiving mail that doesn't do anything for you, and is just taking up space in your inbox, add it to your block list!

- **Create templates for replies that you write frequently.** There's nothing worse than typing the same sentence over and over again

at the start of every single email. If you often
send emails with similar content, consider
making a template that you can copy-paste for
each email. This can be extremely useful if you
deal with lots of different clients. Just
remember to fill in the details after you copy
and paste! This is what I started doing when
my business started demanding a lot of email
time. I noticed a lot of the enquiries were very
similar, so I created templates for my most
popular services. Think of the common
questions you get and spend some time
answering them in a .doc file so that you can
easily access them at any time.

- **Create a FAQs page if necessary.** If you
receive a large amount of emails asking the
same questions from clients over and over, you
may want to include a Frequently Asked
Questions page on your website or blog. You
can redirect people to this page rather than
having to answer the same questions time and
time again. I have a FAQs page on my own
website.

- **Set time limits for reading, as well as writing emails.** Just like spending too much time writing emails can drag you down, spending too much time reading them can be even worse. If you find that you spend a lot of time reading emails when you should just be deleting them and moving on, try setting a timer for two minutes or so. Stop reading when the two minutes is up, then either respond to the email if necessary or delete it.

Best practices

Organizing your emails and reforming your email habits can be as simple as adopting a few new tricks. However, there are a few best practices we can follow to ensure that these steps are easier to take, and work effectively. These practices are also good for staying calm and effective when checking email.

First off, avoid sorting your emails based on topics. This is a common mistake for many people. If you sort emails by topic, you will quickly lose track of which topics need to be handled first, and it will be impossible to properly prioritize your email responses.

Instead, try to make a maximum of 5 folders based around *deadlines.* Sorting your inbox based on when everything needs to be addressed creates a concrete timeline for your email checking and responses. This helps you keep a mental record of which emails need responses and when.

Another thing you want to keep in mind is that *just because you receive a lot of emails, doesn't mean you have more work to do.* Many people see that they're receiving 200, 300, 400 emails each day, and it makes them feel like their workload is increasing. When you actually take the time to tackle these emails in a calm and collected fashion, you will find that the issue is not as urgent as it may seem.

Here's an example of how you could organize your inbox: Let's say that you do content writing for a number of different clients. It doesn't make sense to do projects as you get them, because some of them might need to be finished faster than others. Some of them might also require more work than others. For this scenario, it's probably best to use a deadline-based system. For me, the folder hierarchy would look something like this:

- ☐ Inbox
  - ☐ 2019
    - ☐ November
      - ☐ Draft for client *a*
      - ☐ Draft for client *b*
    - ☐ December
      - ☐ Draft for client *a*
  - ☐ 2020
    - ☐ January
      - ☐ Draft for client *b*
    - ☐ February
      - ☐ Draft for client *a*
  - ☐ 2021
- ☐ Trash

Now, we're going to go over some tips for organizing your inbox in Gmail and Outlook. These are the most popular mail clients, but many of the tips can be used in other email clients as well.

Gmail Tips

Now that we've gone over some steps to help us organize our email habits, let's learn some specific tips for the leading email clients. We'll start with Gmail:

- **Select a layout.** The first order of business with organizing our Gmail inbox is choosing a good layout for what we need to do. In your inbox, click the gear-shaped symbol in the upper-right corner of the screen. Click on "Settings", and then navigate to the "Inbox" tab of the settings window. Here we have a few options for layout:

  - **Default.** The tried-and-true format which organizes your inbox by date received. In this layout, different categories can be selected for the placement of your emails. The categories appear as tabs near the top of the inbox window.

  - **Important First.** This layout automatically attempts to detect important emails and display them first. The ones designated as less important appear lower down on the list.

○ **Unread First.** This layout puts your unread emails at the top, regardless of when they were received. Read emails are sent to the bottom.

○ **Starred First.** This layout will split the inbox into two sections and display your starred emails at the top. Non-starred emails will appear in the bottom section.

○ **Priority Inbox.** This layout will analyze which emails you are most likely to check and respond to based on your past behavior. This ultimately behaves more or less like a combination of all the previous layouts.

○ It's a good idea to try out the different layouts or features and see which one works for you. Some people might find success with one layout while others prefer a different one.

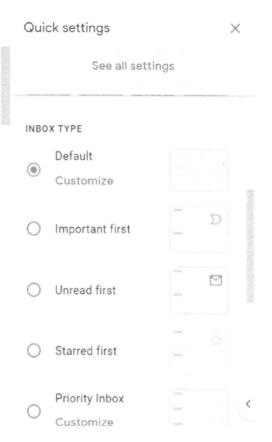

Quick settings   ×

See all settings

INBOX TYPE

⦿   Default
      Customize

○   Important first

○   Unread first

○   Starred first

○   Priority Inbox
      Customize

- **Add a preview pane.** By default, the inbox only shows the sender, subject line, and a tiny blurb of content from the email itself. If you just use this view, you will typically need to open emails in order to see their content. To avoid this, you can add a preview pane to your Gmail inbox.

- Click on the gear in the top right corner of your inbox and select "Settings".

- In the "Settings" window, navigate to the "Labs" tab.

- Scroll down until you see "Preview Pane" and click "enable."

- Don't forget to save your changes!

- **Use custom labels to organize your Gmail. On the left hand side of your inbox window, you probably noticed a list of labels which Gmail uses to organize your different emails.** You can add emails to each label to help Gmail keep your inbox organized, but you can also create custom labels to organize things the way you want.

  - Select a message for which you want to change the label.

  - There is a button near the top of your inbox that looks like a sort of shopping tag. Click on it.

  - From here, you can assign the message to

one of the predefined labels, or you can select "Create New" if you want to make your own label.

- **Create and use custom filters for messages.** In addition to labels for sorting your emails, you can also apply filters to automatically send the messages to the folders where they belong. This is useful for sorting emails without having to manually move each one into a specific folder:

  o Select the emails you wish to filter.

  o Click on the "More" button at the top of your inbox.

  o Select "Filter messages like this" from the

drop-down menu.

- Here, you can choose to filter the messages by sender, subject line, keywords, attachments, and more.

- After deleting how you wish to filter your messages, click "Create filter with this search".

- Now, you can select what you want the filter to actually do with the messages. You can choose to assign custom labels or move the messages to a specific folder.

- Make sure to also select the option to apply the filter to "all conversations" that match the criteria. That way you don't have to create individual filters for each one.

- I use this feature to filter many of my emails and skip the inbox entirely. They each go into a specific folder for me to read later. This makes it much more organized and easier to manage. This can work for specific projects, departments, or types of emails that you receive.

- **Utilize the archive feature.** The archive lets you send specific messages and conversations to a separate folder, where they will only return to your inbox if somebody replies to that conversion. The archive is also automatically deleted after 30 days without any responses to the conversation. You can add a button to automatically archive emails when you reply to a message.

  - Click on the gear icon near the top right hand corner of your inbox.

  - Hit "Settings"

  - Scroll down until you see the "Show 'Send & Archive' option. Turn it on.

  - Don't forget to save your settings!

Outlook tips

Outlook is another popular email client that has been a mainstay for a number of years now (it used to be called *Hotmail*). In general, the same best practices for managing your inbox for Gmail can apply to Outlook as well, but there are a few specific tools we have at our disposal with Outlook that will help us a bit along the way.

- **Keep a To-Do folder for non-urgent emails.** Outlook allows you to create a folder structure for organizing your emails. Adopting a system for organizing your folders is up to you, like we discussed above, but it's always a good idea to have a "to-do" folder for all the emails that you can't get to right away. This is especially useful for trimming down your inbox to just what needs to get done right now.

  - Right click your "Inbox" folder in Outlook.

  - Select "New Folder"

  - Create as many folders as you want and structure them in a logical way.

  - For a "to-do" folder, you might also want to

create subfolders for organizing by date or project.

- **Use the task list.** Setting aside emails for reading them or responding to them at a later time is the basis of how we're organizing our email. In outlook, it helps to set tasks in the task list so that you can be reminded to check and respond to those emails you set aside.

  ○ To assign an email to the task list, click and drag the email over to the task list icon. The icon looks like a small clipboard with a check-mark on it.

  ○ In the task window, you can set a date and time to be reminded about the task.

  ○ If you want to quickly glance at your task list, you can mouse over the task list icon.

  ○ Click on the icon to review the list and the tasks on it.

  ○ Once the reminder is set, it will pop up as a notification from your browser at the set date and time.

  ○ Once the task is complete, open the task

window and double click on the completed
task.

- ○ Click the "Mark Complete" button near the
top to mark the task as completed and
remove it from the task list.

- ○ Try and get into the habit of using the task
list whenever you need to be reminded to
read or respond to a message. Remember to
keep it within your designated email
checking time.

- **Use Outlook's clean-up function.**
Introduced in 2010, Outlook actually has an
automatic cleanup feature that allows you to
clean up your inbox without having to do
everything by hand. This is useful if you've
been on vacation or otherwise haven't checked
your email in a long time. The cleanup tool
actually deletes email replies that are
duplicated later on. This allows you to easily
read singular threads without having to sift
through dozens of emails.

- ○ In your inbox, click the "Clean Up" button.

- In the dropdown menu, select "Clean Up Folder".

- A dialogue box will pop up to confirm the deletion. You can select to not show this message again, if you wish.

- Hit "Clean Up Folder" to finish the cleanup.

- You don't have to worry about accidentally deleting something important. The tool only deletes duplicate content, and you can always check recently deleted items in the trash bin.

- **Use rules to sort your emails automatically.** This works kind of like filters in Gmail. You can set Outlook to identify certain emails and automatically sort them for you to read, respond, or delete later. If you receive a lot of irrelevant mail, this can save you a lot of time sifting through unimportant emails.

  - To create rules, right click on an email.

  - Select "Rules" > "Create Rule"

  - Now you can select the criteria for your

rule.

- ○ To automatically move emails to a folder, select "Move the item to folder", and select the folder where you want those emails to go.

- ○ You can also choose to send them to "deleted items" to delete them automatically.

- ○ Click "OK" to apply.

- **Don't be afraid to ignore threads.** If you've been included in an email thread that doesn't pertain to you or the job you've been tasked with, you can simply choose to ignore the thread so that future replies are not sent to your inbox.

- ○ Right click on the offending email

- ○ Select "Ignore" from the drop down menu.

- ○ Further replies in ignored threads will be automatically sent to the "Deleted Items" folder.

- **Use "Quick Parts" to respond quickly**

and efficiently. This is similar to using stock responses to respond to emails in general, but Outlook has a nifty tool for handling repeated responses. It's Called "Quick Parts". The "Quick Parts" menu allows you to save portions of emails for insertion wherever you want. It even saves things like formatting.

○ Once you've typed a response that you think you will need to use again, high light the section you want to save.

○ Click on the "Insert" tab near the top of the page.

○ In the "Insert" menu, click on "Quick Parts"

○ Select "Save Selection to Quick Part Gallery".

○ Select a descriptive name for your new Quick Part.

○ Click "OK" to confirm.

○ To add the section you just saved to any email, click on "Insert"

○ Navigate to "Quick Parts" and select the

part you wish to insert.

○ Don't forget to tweak the details so that the section you copied matches the current situation.

Outlook has lots of other tools for automating your inbox, more than would be efficient to describe here. For more information, <u>check out this page</u>. The <u>help pages for Outlook</u> can also be a good place to educate yourself on the various tools you have at your disposal.

Tools

Email is a popular form of communication. Accordingly, there are lots of software resources and tools out there that can help you keep things organized without spending too much time or effort. Sifting through all of the available tools to see which ones you should be using can be a bit of a pain, so we'll go over some of the recommended ones here:

• **HubSpot Sales.** This is a Chrome extension that allows you to see who opens your emails, how many times they are opened, and where they are opened from. You can also set automatic notifications for when somebody clicks on one of the links in your email. It integrates quite well with Outlook and Gmail, and is available for free. This is useful if you do a lot of email marketing and have to track the amount of users you have clicking through your email content. It also tracks relevant information about the person to whom you are sending the email. Paid versions are available that allow for automated personal outreach.

- **Shift.** This app allows users to read and send emails from all of their different email accounts with a single program. This is hugely effective if you have separate email accounts for work and for home, or if you use multiple clients for reading and answering emails. This app is also compatible with extensions like HubSpot Sales, Grammarly, and many other popular tools. Shift also includes a search ability that allows you to search all of your email accounts at the same time.

- **Unroll.me.** Unsubscribing from all the newsletters and news reports that you receive is a huge cornerstone of organizing your email. We will go over how to do this in-depth in a moment, but for now we can go over a tool that can help us do it more easily. Unroll.me is a tool that allows you to unsubscribe from all the newsletters that you receive en-masse. You can choose to unsubscribe from every single thing at once, or you can select which specific newsletters from which you wish to unsubscribe.

- **FollowUpThen.** This is a tool that allows you to set reminders for responding to emails, similarly to Outlook's task feature. The difference is that this one also allows you to send automated notifications to your clients to remind *them* to respond. This is useful if you handle teams of people, or regularly deal with multiple clients. This app is free up to 50 reminders per month. This number can be increased with a paid subscription for between $2 and $9 per month. The paid service also includes other features like calendar integration.

There are plenty more tools on the market that help you check emails. Finding the ones that work for you is all about understanding what the market has to offer, and trying things out until you find something that fits. If you need more information or app recommendations, check out this page.

https://blog.hubspot.com/marketing/inbox-organization-tools

Dealing with newsletters and spam

Sometimes it feels like everything we receive is spam. Sometimes we sign up for newsletters thinking that we will be able to use all the information, only to find that the newsletter is more of an annoyance than anything else. Unsubscribing from all of these services is an important step to getting your inbox under control, so let's go over some best practices:

- **When signing up for newsletters, think carefully.** If you are manually signing up for a newsletter, remember that this will *repeatedly* send you emails. Ask yourself if you will really read and make use of this information. Don't sign up for more than a few at a time, max.

- **Create filters for each subscription.** If you receive newsletters that you do like to read and make use of, creating filters to automatically sort each newsletter can be very helpful. This will organize each subscription so that you can get around to reading each one at your own pace. Refer to earlier in the chapter for a guide on how to use filters.

- **Archive or delete newsletters you have read.** Once you're finished reading a newsletter, archive or delete it. There is no sense keeping newsletters around that you have already read. If you want to save some of the information for reference, then consider making notes and keeping them somewhere reasonable on your device.

Adopting these habits will get you used to cutting down on the subscribed content in your email inbox. If you're careful, you should also be able to avoid a lot of spam. Now that we've covered the best practices, let's go a bit more in-depth on how to unsubscribe from newsletters and spam:

- **Use built-in unsubscribe features.** Gmail

has an automated "Unsubscribe" button next to the sender's name in an email that will allow you to unsubscribe from newsletters with just one click. If you are on Android or iOS, open the message and scroll to the bottom to see the "Unsubscribe" button. If you can't find it, look for a similar button within the body of the email.

- **Use *find on page*.** If you hit Ctrl+f (Cmd+f if you're on Mac) on your browser you can type in search terms to find words on your page. You can use this to find unsubscribe buttons within the emails themselves in case the one-click option doesn't work.

- **Use apps or extensions for mass-unsubscribing.** If you have an inordinate number of subscriptions, it's possible that you would benefit from using an app or extension to automatically unsubscribe. This will allow you to tackle the problem of newsletters and spam without having to read through and unsubscribe from individual lists. Unroll.me is a great tool that we talked about earlier in the chapter for this purpose. A good alternative to Unroll.me is Mailstrom.

Summary

Organizing your email inbox and keeping it that way can be a bit of a challenge, but with the right tools and knowledge, any task can be completed:

- **Limit your email time.** Set concrete times for checking your email. Limit yourself to twice a day, set time limits, and don't check your email outside this window.

- **Write concisely.** The best emails are short and sweet while still having all the necessary information. Learn to write more concisely so that you spend less time sending emails back-and-forth.

- **Sort your inbox.** Use folders, filters, labels, and other tools to keep your inbox organized.

- **Use templates.** If you type the same responses over and over again, use templates and pre-set messages to save time when responding.

- **Gmail.** Use labels, select a proper layout, and configure your filters to keep your inbox organized.

- **Outlook.** Use the task list, clean-up tool, rules, and quick parts to help organize your inbox and respond to emails efficiently.

- **Unsubscribe from newsletters.** Manage the subscriptions you have and unsubscribe from the ones you don't need.

For the next chapter, we'll be taking a look at our social media accounts and how to organize our lives so that we don't spend so much time on social media.

Chapter 5: Social Media

"The first rule of social media is that everything changes all the time. What won't change is the community's desire to network."

-Kami Huyse

In 2006, when I was in my first year of university, there was this hot new app spreading around that allowed you to easily add others to your list of friends. That app was Facebook. I remember how exciting it was to add new content to my profile and update my status. My friends list grew larger over time, and I felt a sense of pride having made so many friends. It was a great way to stay in touch and see what people were doing.

However, as time went on, I began to spend more and more time on Facebook. Eventually, I was spending more time browsing Facebook than I did studying or working. Facebook had become a huge time sink for me. It was difficult to keep up with everything on my news feed; there was always more information waiting for me to read about people and the world around me.

I started noticing that I was comparing myself to others more often. Everyone else seemed to be leading amazing lives. They were all taking vacations, buying new cars or houses, and going to events while I was stuck at home working or studying. Over time it became just so... *depressing*. After a while, I realized that I wasn't even talking to most of the people with whom I had made "friends" on Facebook.

It has become almost mechanical to ask people if they have Facebook for you to add. Now we do it because we *should*, not because we want to. And then, we often add each other and then never speak to each other again. I knew that I had to take control of my life and reign in my time spent on Facebook. If I didn't it would end up controlling my life!

Nowadays, I only go on Facebook to check a couple of author groups of which I am a part; or to keep in touch with a few close friends. I've actually installed a Google Chrome extension that blocks out the newsfeed on Facebook, displaying an inspirational quote instead. I've also been limiting myself to only checking Facebook after I finish my work around 7PM, and only for 20 minutes.

Statistics and overview

Understanding the numbers behind social media usage is instrumental to understanding the influence that it has on our lives. First off, Emarsys reports that *3.5 billion* people use social media *every day*. That's roughly 45% of the world's population. This number has expanded dramatically in recent years as platforms become more accessible and integrated with the world around us.

Secondly, across those 3.5 billion people, each one spends an average of *3 hours per day* browsing social media and messaging apps, as reported by Global Web Index. That's a huge network of people, and an area with huge potential if you're in marketing. If you're simply looking at cat pictures, however, this is a huge waste of your time.

Lastly, Hootsuite reports that 99% of social media users in 2019 accessed from mobile devices. This means that the overwhelming majority of people are actually checking their social media from their pocket as they are out-and-about. While this creates unique opportunities for marketing, it also means that most users never really escape the net of social media.

Social media addiction

All of the factors I mentioned above contribute to *social media addiction.* While we might like to think that social media addiction is something that only affects a few people across the world, the reality is actually far worse. Most social media users express some form of addictive behavior. This comes as no surprise, since social media is free and accessible; it's easy to get the validation that we crave in our day-to-day lives. The important thing to remember is that *nothing is free...* especially if you are paying with your time and attention.

Feeling validated on a social level is a basic human necessity. Humans are social creatures, and in a properly functioning society, social interaction forms a huge part of day-to-day life, as well as the inner monologue and psyche of the population.

In today's world however, scientists, businesses, and

developers have identified all of the different cues that our brains use to drive social validation. They have learned to synthesize it so that they can provide this validation to us as a service, rather than have us interact with each other organically to feel validated. This works primarily through what scientists call *the reward pathway*.

Social media is designed to imitate the aspects of our social lives that cause us to feel validated. They do this by triggering a rush of endorphins known as a *dopamine high*. This is a reward mechanism that your brain uses to teach you what around you is good and desirable. When used against you, it can induce learned behaviors that are harmful and unproductive, such as browsing social media for three hours every single day.

General tips for social media management

The negative effects of social media addiction can be alleviated by taking control of your social media usage. The problem is that most people have become accustomed to experiencing that dopamine rush they get when they use social media. This is that "bored" feeling you get that makes you want to take out your phone. Learning to catch ourselves and redirect that energy into something more constructive is the basis of effective social media management.

Since social media is constantly evolving, many specific things about social media management will change over time. However, there are generally a few good tips you can follow to cut down on your social media time:

- **Use apps to limit screen time.** There are plenty of apps out there that you can use to limit your screen time. Whether it is a simple reminder to log off, or an app that actually locks you out of certain websites, using these tools can greatly increase your chances of staying off social media. We'll talk more about social media management apps in a moment, but some good recommendations include Apple's *Screen Time* (Accessed through the settings menu on your phone), or Google's *Digital Wellbeing*.

- **Set limits on the time of day that you use social media.** If you simply log on and off of social media whenever you want, you will have a hard time controlling yourself, and you will probably end up browsing for longer than you intended. You might even procrastinate to the point where you spend the entire day on social media and get nothing done. Making sure to finish important tasks *before* using social media can help combat this effect. Try setting a specific time for when you can start using social media after work. Specific times are easier to stick to, and provide a concrete sense of progress.

- **Do a social media "detox".** If you feel that "itch" of social media addiction, and it is distracting you or making it very difficult to cut back on your screen time, it might be a good idea to do a social media detox. We'll talk about this more in-depth later on in the chapter, but it's important to remember that staying away from social media for at least 7 days will rehabilitate your brain to use it less. This strategy can be used for other things, as well, such as cutting down on added sugar in your diet.

- **Try utilizing greyscale.** Greyscale is exactly what it sounds like. Most devices have the option to display content in greyscale as an accessibility option for people who have trouble perceiving color. The cool thing about this is that removing color from social media neuters its ability to trigger your reward pathways. Looking at Instagram with no colors is boring, and that's a good thing!

- **Turn off notifications.** If your social media accounts are sending you notifications every time one of your friends posts something on their story, then you will constantly be reminded that you're missing out on social media content. Turning off notifications will ensure that you can stay on task much easier. Out of sight; out of mind.

- **Set aside a day of the week for avoiding screen time.** Pick a day where you won't be too busy, and set that day as a "social-media-free" day. Try to limit your screen time as much as possible. If you make this into a habit, your brain will get more used to existing without the constant validation of social media. Eventually, you will learn to be satisfied simply with the world around you.

- **Try going cold turkey.** If you still have a lot of trouble putting your phone down and staying away from social media, then going cold turkey might be a good idea for you. This means actually turning off your phone and putting it somewhere you can't access it. Giving your devices to a friend for safekeeping works quite well for this strategy. Since your brain won't be able to get the instant gratification that it desires from social media, it will be forced to change its expectations and rehabilitate your reward pathways.

Apps to reduce your screen time

Once you've adopted some measures to help yourself get away from social media, you will probably find that certain strategies help more than others. Everybody is different, and the ways in which we interact with social media and the world around us are different as well. If you are having trouble tracking your social media time and effectively taking measures to curb it, there are a large number of apps out there that could be useful for you.

First of all, most smartphones have modes or apps that allow you to block or disable apps you want to stay away from without uninstalling them. Focus Time is a good example. Another good way to help cut back on your social media time is to turn off the internet connection on your device, or putting the device away in a drawer. The idea is to lock yourself out of your addiction to put obstacles to put between yourself and relapse.

- **Offtime.** This is an app for blocking out all the most distracting apps on your phone. You can even block out text messages, if you so desire. This app also allows you to set times when certain apps can and cannot be used. This is useful for automating the social media time that you've allowed yourself.

- **Moment.** This is a simple app for tracking the time you spend on your device each day. The app tracks how much you use each app, and you can set notifications at specific times to cut down on areas where you are spending too much of your time and effort. There is also an option to set up a Moment system for the whole family at once, allowing you to get your family involved with your social media rehabilitation.

- **Flipd.** This app works similarly to Offtime, but in a much more serious capacity. Flipd allows you to set times and locks on your various apps, as well as track time used on them. Once you lock yourself out of an app with Flipd, there is no going back, so make sure you know what you're doing before you proceed.

- **Freedom.** This app actually uses a Virtual Protocol Network (VPN) to stop social media apps from receiving any updates. This is an effective way to stop social media apps and other distractions from making their way into your sphere. You can even use it to block things like text messages and emails.

- **Appbloc.** This is a nice alternative that allows you to set times for being locked out of specific apps. Unfortunately, it does not also have a time tracking feature, but it would work in tandem with another app for tracking your usage, such as Moment.

- **Selfcontrol.** SelfControl is an app for Macintosh that gives you the ability to block access to websites, email, and anything else on your computer that could be distracting to you. You can also set specific times for locking out certain websites. It will take a bit to set up your blacklist, but this is a great option for mac users who spend a lot of time checking social media online.

Managing Facebook

Getting away from Facebook can be quite the task. Sometimes, even when we want to log off of social media and do something else, we find ourselves checking Facebook on our phones without even realizing it. This is the feedback loop created by Facebook developers working with mountains of data about how its users behave. Luckily, it *is* possible to free yourself from this loop.

- **Try going messenger-only.** Many people

continue using Facebook simply because it is expected of them. Many people use Facebook as their primary means of communication, particularly within their social circle. This is what keeps many people logging onto Facebook even if they aren't interested in checking their feed. If you want to avoid endless Facebooking, but you still need to send and receive messages, consider using Facebook Messenger as a standalone application. You can download it as an app for mobile or simply use the standalone website (https://www.messenger.com/). There is also *Messenger Lite*, which is an even more stripped-down version of messenger to save space on your device.

- **Unfollow everything.** Okay, not *everything*, but if you take a good look at all of the pages you are following on social media, you will probably notice that there are some things that you don't really care about. Cutting down on the amount of pages you follow will trim the clutter from your feed and allow you to spend less time browsing Facebook. If you are really serious about cutting down your social media time, try unfollowing *every* page that doesn't directly enrich your life in some way. There are also browser extensions that allow you to unfollow things en-masse and remove them from your news feed, such as *Unfollow Everything*.

- **Use a different browser.** This tip is useful for staying on task when you want to avoid social media. The more you use Facebook on one browser, the more that browser learns about the way you behave, and the more integrated with Facebook data collection your behavior becomes. Using a different browser for work compared to social media can help you avoid being dragged back onto Facebook.

- **Remove links and default tabs.** If you have quick links to Facebook on your bar, or a default tab open to Facebook at all times, it will obviously cause you to fall back into checking Facebook more often. Remove extra buttons and try to keep your default tabs as minimalistic as possible.

There are lots of things you can do to help curb the time you spend on Facebook. Eventually, you will be less inclined to check it, and you will feel much more free and productive. One of the best tools I use for managing Facebook usage is *News Feed Eradicator*. This app actually removes your news feed and replaces it with inspirational messages.

Managing other platforms

There are tons of social media platforms out there, and each one presents its own challenges for managing our time and productivity. Since these platforms are constantly changing, it is beyond the scope of this book to address them all, but we can go over some basic tips and tricks for each:

- **Twitter.** Just like with Facebook, twitter creates a kind of infinite loop of feedback. Breaking this loop is essential to reducing your time spent on twitter. The key for twitter is mainly to disable notifications and unsubscribe from most of the accounts you're following. You don't really need to know what all your favorite celebrities are thinking at this exact moment. Apple's *Screen Time* app is a good tool for this if you're using iOS or MacOS devices. For Android, there's a great app you can use called *Appdetox.*

- **Instagram.** Instagram is one of the most insidious apps on the market. The developers have managed to create an entire subculture based around watching glorified advertisements during every spare moment of your day. This is where greyscale is one of your best friends, as it can curb the effect that Instagram has on your brain. Ask yourself: *is the media I see on Instagram improving my* *life in any way, shape, or form?* If Instagram isn't improving your life, then uninstall it. Block the website from your browsers. Spend that time reading a book or going outside. If you used Instagram to watch cooking videos, learn to actually cook. In August of 2018, Facebook and Instagram announced that they had introduced new features to help people limit their social media time. To access these tools, go to the settings page on Instagram. Tap on "Your Activity", and you will be shown a dashboard that displays the average time you spend on that app for the device you're using. From here you can set daily reminders. You can also mute push notifications from this menu.

- **Snapchat.** Snapchat can be a fun way to interact with your friends, but it can also be a huge time sink. The key to cutting down on time spent snapchatting is to properly curate your contact list. Only communicate with a small circle of close friends, and limit your time spent using Snapchat to a specific time of day, and only for a little bit at a time. There is a great app for monitoring and controlling your Snapchat usage called *FamiSafe*. This is originally intended as a parental control app for monitoring and limiting children's social media usage. However, the reminder settings and app lock options make it work just fine for limiting your time on Snapchat.

- **YouTube.** Once you create an account and start curating playlists and subscriptions, YouTube can quickly suck you in so that you spend hours watching videos. The easiest way to curb this is to delete your account and only use the site for watching specific videos. There used to be a way to disable recommended videos on YouTube, *but they removed it.* That should tell you all you need to know about their motivations. There are also browser extensions for managing your YouTube subscriptions and time spent watching videos. *YouTube Mass Unsubscribe* allows you to unsubscribe from all your channels at once.

There are many more social media platforms out there that can be tackled in their own ways, but making a list of each one is beyond the scope of this book.

Procrastination

We all know what it feels like to procrastinate. You can sit there all day checking your messages, thinking about your work, but never actually doing it. The longer you wait, the harder it gets; and suddenly the deadline approaches and you have to stay up until the Nth hour just to finish your work.

Stop Procrastinating, an app that allows users to disconnect and stop wasting time, actually conducted some research based on their app to try and figure out the root of procrastination. What they found is hardly surprising: social media usage accounts for the vast majority of people's procrastination. 75% of students surveyed reported that they had lost their train of thought while studying due to social media, compares to only 17% reporting television as the cause.

Aside from using apps and such to disconnect yourself from social media (which we'll talk about in a moment), procrastinating is mainly a problem of habits. Most of us try to work towards long-term rewards such as graduation or landing a job.

Goalsetting is important, but you need to have short-term habits which reward your brain in order to keep it on track.

The key is to recognize where you become distracted, and what motivates you to procrastinate. Once you have an understanding of these things, it's easier to employ best practices in order to manage your time better.

Best practices

Now that we've gone over some of the practical solutions for cutting down on social media time, let's go over some best practices that we can adopt to help keep ourselves off of social media:

- **Limit data usage.** Since most people will be connecting with wifi, placing limits on your data can help you cut down on social media when you're out and about. Try to set a reasonable limit that allows you to perform necessary tasks while making it hard for you to browse aimlessly for hours.

- **Read or listen to audiobooks.** Rather than checking your phone when you're bored on the subway, take out a book and start reading. You can listen to audiobooks, as well, if that's more your speed. If you're *really* serious about self-improvement, limit yourself to non-fiction or classical works. You can download Kindle ebooks directly from Amazon, or audiobooks from Audible. You can also find both ebooks and audiobooks on Overdrive. Don't forget that one of the best places for free reading material is the good old local library!

- **Use those apps.** There's no sense downloading a bunch of apps to manage your time and limit social media usage if you never actually use them. Set aside time before using social media to set up limits with your apps. Use the time afterwards to examine the time you spent and how well you spent it.

- **Downgrade your phone.** You can't check social media with a simple flip phone. Downgrading to a flip phone or something similar is a great way to escape the loop of constantly checking your phone for updates. This also allows you to continue communicating by text with the people in your life who actually matter.

- **Stick to your cut-off time.** There's no sense in setting a cut-off time for your social media usage if you don't stick to it. Remember to set timers and alarms if necessary, and don't be afraid to use apps for limiting your time spent, or putting your mobile device somewhere where it won't distract you. I personally set an alarm for 10PM to remind myself to turn off all my data and phones for the night. If anybody needs to reach me in case of emergencies, they can send a text message.

These are similar to the general tips we discussed earlier in the chapter. Feel free to give yourself time to unwind; it's not productive to spend *all* of your time working and getting burned out. That being said, you can definitely spend your time doing something more practical than browsing social media.

You could watch a documentary, read a book, or even start learning a new language. With things like Netflix at our disposal, it can be quite easy to sit around and watch for hours on end, or playing video games for hours trying to reach the next level. Believe me, I've been there.

Instead of trying to escape from your life with movies or games, try to use your spare time to improve yourself and try new things. Limiting the time you spend watching Netflix or playing video games also allows you to use these things as rewards when you complete your work. Just make sure you limit yourself like watching one episode of your favourite show after working out at the gym for at least an hour.

Don't forget to set timers for your breaks, as well. It helps to get in the rhythm of knowing exactly when your break is over. I can enjoy myself and then return to work once the alarm goes off. I also limit my T.V. time until after 8PM-10PM after I finish my work.

Summary

- **Use apps to limit your social media time.** There are plenty of apps out there that can automatically cut you off from social media if you're spending too much time on it.

- **Set limits and stick to them.** Give yourself specific limits for when and where you can use social media. Sticking to these limits will teach your brain to depend less on social media.

- **Use greyscale.** Try setting your apps to appear in greyscale so that the colors are less attractive for your brain.

- **Turn off notifications.** Don't let social media reach you when you're trying to stay away from it. Disable notifications to avoid temptation and stay on task.

- **set a no-screen day.** Set aside one of the less busy days of the week for staying away from all screens. Go outside; read a book; do some exercises.

- **Cold turkey/detox.** If you have a serious social media addiction, cutting yourself off entirely for a little bit might be what it takes to rehabilitate your brain.

- **Manage Facebook.** Limit your usage and remove yourself from the things on Facebook that drag you back every time. Use apps to disable things like the newsfeed.

- **Manage your other apps.** Different social media platforms all present different challenges for you to overcome. Do some research and read up on the best ways to approach each one.

- **Read or listen to audiobooks.** Rather than spending all your free time browsing social media or chatting with friends; try to educate yourself by reading a book or listening to audiobooks.

- **Stick with it.** None of this will matter if you can't stick with it. If you fall back into old habits, don't worry about it. Just pick yourself up and try again.

In the next chapter, we'll be taking an in-depth look at managing our time and coexisting with technology and social media so that we can lead productive and fulfilling lives.

Chapter 6: Time Management and Productivity

"Strive not to be a success, but to be of value."

-Albert Einstein

Before I took control of my life, I was always late to meetings with others. I always felt rushed, like there wasn't enough time in a day. I would always wait until the last minutes to complete assignments at school, and I would often have to pull all-nighters to compensate for lost time. I felt constantly stressed.

I'm sure many of you reading this have felt this way before, too. With all the noise and clutter in our lives today, it isn't surprising that many people find themselves in these situations or similar ones every day. However, after working on my time management skills, I feel much more in control.

Nowadays, I am rarely late, and I often show up early to appointments and meetings. Especially when working online, I like to schedule and plan things ahead of time. This way, I can ensure that I have enough time to complete all the necessary tasks. I like to know exactly what I need to do.

Focus on one thing

The American Psychological Association reports that multiple studies from the late 90's and early 2000's examined productivity and multitasking to find the secret behind human productivity. What they found was that trying to multitask is one of the *worst* things you can do for your productivity. Most people think about productivity in terms of doing *more* things, when in reality human beings are far more productive when they can focus on just *one* thing.

Of course, many of us have schedules that are chock full of different tasks. It can be hard to break down our schedules so that we can focus on one thing at a time. Luckily enough, there are a few ways that we can make things easier for ourselves.

The 20/80 rule

The 20/80 rule is a concept first postulated by Italian economist Vilfredo Pareto. It is sometimes referred to as *Pereto's Principle*. What the 20/80 rule suggests is that *80% of results in most contexts come from roughly 20% of the causes*. This principle is surprisingly consistent throughout many aspects of economics, business, and even nature. Here are some examples:

- Most people tend to wear 20% of their wardrobe 80% of the time.

- 20% of the world possesses roughly 80% of the world's wealth.

- 80% of flowers that bloom result from roughly 20% of the seeds that were planted.

These are just examples to demonstrate the principle. The fact is that this rule extends to human behavior and productivity, as well. The point of this observation is not specifically to make you work less, but to realize that most of the *results* from your work only come from a small fraction of all the effort you put in. *Input and output is not proportional.*

What this means is that you need to make your efforts count. Spending all of your time switching between different tasks means that you will never be focusing your efforts on any one task. If you do this, not only will your work suffer, but *you* will suffer as well.

Work in 25/5 or 50/10

Francesco Cirillo, a professional consultant, devised a system in the 1980's that he called the *pomodoro technique*. Basically, humans tend to be more productive when they work in short bursts with breaks in between to keep their minds refreshed. The traditional *pomodoro* (Italian for "tomato", from the tomato-shaped timer Cirillo himself used for the technique), consists of 25 minutes of work with a 5 minute break in between. It is also recommended to take a longer break every 4 periods or so.

You want each period to focus on a specific task. If you are doing tasks that require longer periods, 50 minute work periods with 10 minute breaks is a good way to do it. If you finish a task before the period is up, you should spend the remaining time reflecting on how well you completed the task, and if there is anything you can do to improve.

A typical pomodoro routine would look something like this:

1. Break your task down into workable chunks, and think about how much time you need for each chunk.

2. Set a timer for how long you need. A good rule of thumb is 25 minutes for each period.

3. Start the timer and work until it rings. If you finish your chunk with time to spare, take the remaining time to reflect on how you did and how you can improve.

4. Set the timer for five minutes and take a break from working. Try to do something stimulating that won't distract you too much in between work periods. If you took longer than 25 minutes, longer breaks are a good idea.

5. Rinse and repeat, after 4 work periods, take an extended break to refresh yourself before returning to step one.

6. Repeat the process until the task is complete or the day is done. Learning to walk away is just as important as staying on task.

Learn to say "no"

Some people find it very difficult to refuse when others ask for things. Others find it difficult to say no when invited to hang out with co-workers or friends. This is all well and good, but it can be a huge thorn in your side in terms of time-management. If you are always spending time taking on extra work, or going out with friends, then it will be very difficult for you to establish and follow an effective routine.

The key to overcoming this is learning to say "no". Whether it be for taking on extra tasks at work, or going out with friends. Obviously, it's not always a good idea to say no at work, so being reasonable is an important thing to keep in mind. For hanging out with friends, try to set an achievable goal, such as "this week I will not go out with friends". Setting aside a specific day or time for social activities helps manage this, as well.

Learn to schedule your time

Effective time management is driven by effective scheduling. It's impossible to focus on any task if you spend your time moving between tasks randomly. For this reason, it is essential to learn how to make effective schedules for your day, week, month, and beyond. If you're not used to scheduling, then it can take a few tries before you get it right, but there are some general steps you can follow to start yourself on the right track:

1. Make a list of everything you need to do in a day. It's alright if you start with a rough list and then revise it later. Be thorough; include things like time to eat, time to commute, time spent working, grooming, sleeping, and anything else you need to do in a day.

2. Examine the list and determine how long each task will require. Don't worry about the order of the tasks for right now, just try and be honest and realistic about how long you will need for each task.

3. Determine which tasks from your list are 100% necessary. Typically, you can identify a few tasks which are less important or urgent than others. Categorizing your lists like this is important, because it helps you keep track of important tasks and potentially eliminate less

important ones.

4. Plan out your day. Start with the most important tasks. Keep deadlines in mind for projects, and make sure you're giving yourself enough time to complete each task sufficiently. Leave some wiggle room in between tasks to account for little variations. If you pack everything in too tightly, you will fall behind and start to feel like you aren't getting things done.

5. Once you've worked out a rough idea for your schedule, examine it to see if there's anything you can change. Typically, some of the tasks will be more efficient if grouped together, such as running errands in the same part of town where you buy your groceries.

6. Check your schedule frequently throughout the day. This allows you to stay on track, as well as reflect on how well your schedule is working out for you. If you start falling behind, don't sweat it; just continue working through it. You can always improve on your schedule-making going forward.

7. Do this every day, and make sure to give yourself time to reflect on how you can improve your scheduling and time management. Over time, you will start to form regular habits around scheduling, and might even be able to use schedule "templates" for different days of the week.

Weekly and monthly planning

Once you've gotten into the groove of scheduling and learning to manage your time, it will become easier to take a step back and look towards some long-term goals. The principles for long-term goal setting are similar for daily scheduling. The key is to properly reflect on what you want to accomplish, and break that goal into smaller, actionable tasks.

- **Outline your big plans.** Try planning out the next week of your life. Don't worry about your detailed daily schedules right now, just think about what long-term goals you might want to accomplish this week. Think about the different things that need to get done in order to accomplish this goal, and think about where in your week it most makes sense to schedule these tasks.

- **Fill in the details.** Once you've got an idea for the big-ticket items in your weekly schedule, you can work out the detailed daily routines around your weekly goal. You can be as detailed as you want for this step, as long as you aren't getting distracted by the little things. Remember to keep your long-term goal in mind.

- **Check your plan regularly.** Check your weekly plan at least once a day, and reflect on how well you are doing on working towards your long-term goals. Again, if you are falling behind, don't sweat it too much. Identifying problems is one of the reasons to reflect on your planning. It's useful to reflect at the end of the week on how well you did, as well.

- **Rinse and repeat.** When the week is over, make some notes on how you can improve, and then start again. Over time, you can extend your planning for longer-term goals over months or even years. When you reflect on each week, you will be able to see how far you've come. The key is to stick with it.

Invest in a whiteboard or calendar

There are plenty of tools out there for time management, but sometimes the old fashioned way is still the best. Keeping a whiteboard or calendar for making notes and planning your schedule is a great way to visually keep track of information. Calendars also help you keep track of time as it passes so you don't feel like your days are blurring together.

If you prefer, there are also digital white board tools such as Trello which allow you to keep track of tasks digitally. This is especially useful for tracking tasks in teams, but can also be useful just for planning and managing your personal time.

Hire a virtual assistant, if you have the resources

There are droves of freelancers and other digital professionals working over the internet who would be happy to help you with various administrative or repetitive tasks. Hiring virtual assistants (VAs) can be an immense help, especially if you are running your own successful business.

This is less of an option for people who have less resources at their disposal, but you would be surprised how cheap some of these services can actually be. If you shop around on freelance work boards online, such as UpWork or Freelancer, you might be able to find somebody who can help you out.

Outsourcing your work is a great way to cover ground that would normally give you trouble. This is very common in many industries, like hiring temp workers to cover less important tasks in an office, or comic book artists hiring an intern to draw the backdrops of their comic books. Outsourcing as much as possible ensures that you can focus on a few key tasks in your schedule rather than having to work around dozens of smaller tasks.

When I first started my business, I was basically doing everything on my own. I was working with a tight budget, and I needed the experience, so this was manageable for a while. However, my business began to grow, and looking back on it now, I probably should have started outsourcing my work much earlier. Nowadays, I hire people to help me with cover designs, editing, content, marketing, you name it. If I had to do all of this myself, it would take me much longer to complete these tasks, and it probably wouldn't get done with the same level of quality.

Being able to outsource my work had freed up a lot of my time, allowing me to work on more important things and focus my efforts on different areas of my life. It also feels good to help other people as well as the economy. I highly suggest trying to outsource as much as possible once you can afford to do so.

Review your goals often

The cornerstone of good time management is goal setting. If you don't have goals to work toward, you will never see the "light at the end of the tunnel" so to speak, and you will get bogged down feeling like you never accomplish anything.

Good goals follow the S.M.A.R.T. principles:

- **Specific.** Effective goals must be specific, like "I want to exercise three times a week". Having generic goals like "lose weight" are too vague to be effective.

- **Measurable.** Good goals can be measured.

This helps you understand how well you are doing at achieving them. This is an extension of being specific. A measurable goal would be something like "run 5 kilometers today". If your goal is something like "become a better golfer", then you won't ever really know whether or not you've accomplished it.

- **Achievable.** It's no use setting goals that are impossible for you to achieve. Make sure that your goals can be realistically achieved. If you cannot achieve your goals, then you will constantly be disappointed. "Solving world hunger" is a noble idea, but as a goal, it is a bit too far-fetched to be effective. A good "achievable" goal is something like "Exercise three times this week".

- **Relevant.** Your goals should be relevant to your efforts. If you're making goals for improving your health, but you include things like "attend night classes", then your goals will be unfocused and less effective. If you're trying to lose weight, for example, a good relevant goal would be "Stay under 2000 calories a day for a week".

- **Time-sensitive.** Your goals should be limited to specific periods of time. There's no sense in setting a goal for yourself without giving yourself a deadline. Having time-sensitive deadlines for your goals ensures that you have to work toward them regularly and effectively. Don't forget to be reasonable about your deadlines! You will get more used to how long you need to complete certain tasks as you get experienced in your routine. A good example of a time-sensitive goal would be something like "Finish up my term paper by the end of the day tomorrow".

These goals tend to work best when you take time to reflect on them and how well you are achieving them. Set aside time at the end of your day to review your daily goals, as well as at the end of the week, month, or even year for reviewing your long-term goals.

Apps for time management

Using the scheduling and timer apps on your phone will often be enough for getting things done, but there are plenty of apps on the market that can help you manage your time even more efficiently:

- **Trello.** Trello is an app that allows you to organize your thoughts, schedules, and tasks on a virtual bulletin board. This gives you a visual way of managing your time and effort. I personally use this app on a daily basis for organizing my day, my week, and my projects.

- **Evernote.** This is a notebook app that allows you to save basically anything as a note in your phone. You can store text files, checklists, reminders, and even things like screenshots or images of documents. You can also tag entries to help keep your notes organized. The app can be synced between your mobile device and your laptop, allowing you to plan things on both devices.

- **Pocket.** This app allows you to save articles and links and other materials for later perusal. This is great if you see a headline during the day that interests you, but you don't have time to read it right at the moment. I frequently save articles that seem interesting in order to read them later, it helps me save time when I should be doing something more important than reading articles. It also allows me to archive information that might be relevant to me later on.

- **Todoist.** This is a checklist app that allows you to track tasks over time. You set to-do lists and check off tasks as you do them. At the end of your day or week, the app will show you how much you've accomplished over time. This is great for reflecting on how effective your time management efforts are.

Summary

- **Focus on one thing.** Humans are most productive when they can focus on one task, rather than switching between multiple tasks.

- **Remember the 20/80 rule.** 80% of results come from roughly 20% of your effort. Focus your efforts to make them more effective.

- **Outsource whenever possible.** Hire a virtual assistant or outsource some of your tasks to a freelancer or agency. Lightening your load is one of the most effective time management strategies.

- **Set and review your goals. Goal setting** is the cornerstone of effective time management. Use SMART goal setting principles and reflect on your goals often.

- **Use apps to help you manage your time.** There are plenty of apps on the market to help people manage their tasks and effort. Try out a few and see if you can't find one that works for you.

In the next chapter, we'll be going over various ways to lead a more enriching life.

Chapter 7: How to live a more enriching life

"The joy in life is his who has the heart to demand it."

-Theodore Roosevelt

At the beginning of this book, I mentioned that I wanted to share the success and happiness that I had achieved with others. This is still very true, and the end-goal for digital de-cluttering is eventually the ability to lead a more fulfilling life. Why go through all this trouble if it wasn't going to make you happy?

Of course, de-cluttering our devices and habits with social media and the internet is a good start, but it won't be enough to truly make our lives more enriching. There are a number of ways we need to change our habits and thinking if we want to make the most of our lives.

30-day digital detox

We talked about this a little bit in the social media chapter, but now we're going to go a bit more in-depth with a digital detox plan for *all* of our online habits. Undertaking a detox like this will reduce the dependence your brain has on social media and the internet, allowing you to focus your energy and time on making yourself feel happier and more fulfilled.

- **Preparing for your detox.** There are a few things you want to get out of the way *before* you start doing your detox, in order to give yourself the best possible chances for success.

  ○ Write down your goals and ideas for your detox period. If you go into this not knowing what you want to accomplish, then you won't have a way of knowing if you succeeded.

  ○ Gather and configure any apps you will be using for your digital detox. Set timers and read over reference materials so that you can spend as little time as possible using social media or the internet during your detox.

  ○ Tell people about your detox and/or give yourself a fail safe. Telling people about your plans to detox from the internet will give you a support system to help you get through it.

○ Make a list of things that you will still need to use the internet for during your detox. *You will only be using the internet for these specific things.*

• **During your detox.** This is where things will get a bit difficult. You have to actually remove yourself from your bad habits and begin detoxing from social media and the internet.

○ **The first day**. This will probably be the hardest one for you if you're just starting out. The first thing you will want to do is log off of your social media and devices. Lock yourself out using apps that limit your screen time. Make sure you have a schedule of other tasks to keep you busy during your detox.

○ **The first week.** After a few days have passed, you will probably fall into a routine of keeping yourself away from social media and the internet. You will also begin to see the areas where you have trouble staying on task, or even falling into old habits. The key to succeeding past the one-week mark is to stay vigilant.

- Take time at the end of the week to reflect on how well you did with your digital detox. Brainstorm some changes that you can make to help yourself be more successful staying away from social media. Check in with your support system and let them know how you've been doing.

○ **The rest of it.** This is where your reflection will pay off big time. If you were serious about examining what was working and not working for you during the first week, you will see results from that reflection in the remaining time for your detox.

- Keep up with your habits and checking in with your support system. At this point, you should be forming new habits around habits other than social media. It should be easier and easier as time goes on to stay off of the internet and avoid checking your twitter page etc.

- If you're still having difficulty, don't sweat it. Take a breather, review how far you've come, and try to think of ways to make yourself more successful. Consult your support group and see if they have any ideas to share with you.

○ **After your detox.** This period is possibly the most important part of your digital detox. Now that you've gone 30 days with drastically reduced social media and internet time, you should take a step back and reflect on how successful you were.

- Identify new habits that you have developed. Whether you spent that extra time reading books or learning a new language, identify the new habits that you formed during your digital detox.

- Think about all the things you *didn't* do during your detox. Think about all the times you *wanted* to check your Facebook or Twitter page, but you managed to control yourself. It wasn't *that* bad, was it? What made it difficult? What made it easy? How can you internalize this experience as you move forward out of your detox period?

Deep Work

Cal Newport, the Associated Professor of Computer Science at Georgetown University, has authored six self-improvement books focused on something he calls *Deep Work*. To put it simply, Deep Work is the ability that human beings have allowing them to focus intensely on a task that demands a lot of their effort or attention. It's a kind of focusing exercise that allows you to teach yourself complex skills or complete huge amounts of work effectively within a small amount of time.

If you know what it feels like to spend hour after hour customizing your social media pages and collecting likes, then you know what deep work feels like. The problem is that many people put this kind of focused energy toward things that they don't need. The idea is to take that same level of focus that most people put into killing time, and put it towards something that matters.

Another way of thinking about this is the concept of "flow". This is a concept postulated by renowned psychologist, Mihaly Csikszentmihalyi. Csikszentmihalyi famously examined "optimal experiences" of his subjects, noting that human beings tend to enter an almost trance like state of continuous stimulation when they are doing something they enjoy. This focused energy can be harnessed and put towards more productive goals. It also helps people experience deep fulfillment and increased creativity.

You can see what I mean if you work towards something that matters to you. Developing your "flow" and taking advantage of it is easiest with something that you enjoy doing, but is still challenging enough to be engaging and stretch your mental focus. Try thinking of hobbies that you like or used to be involved in. Perhaps you enjoy painting, playing an instrument, studying a language, or any number of things. Set aside some time to engage in that activity and really lose yourself. Feel how focused you become when you enjoy what you're doing and learn to harness that energy.

Mindfulness and living an enriched life.

Feeling enriched by your life requires more than just changing habits. You need to adopt the right mindset in order to *allow yourself to be happy.* De-cluttering our digital lives is a good start, but there a few more steps we should take to ensure that we are getting the most out of our lives:

- **Realize it's okay to be bored.** Social media addiction is driven by the sense that being bored is the worst thing in the world. What we need to realize is that being bored is a natural state for humans, which normally drives them to accomplish things. If you constantly appease your boredom with simple instant-gratification, you will never improve. Learning to live with boredom and flourish with it is essential to living a fulfilling life.

- **Find time for yourself.** If you spend all your time working or completing necessary tasks, you will quickly become burned out and fall back into bad habits. Scheduling "me time" for yourself is essential to keeping your mind and body working properly. Try setting aside some time at the end of your day/week/month to reflect and spend time doing something you enjoy, like reading a book or practicing an instrument.

- **Live in the moment.** We often spend all of our time worrying about future events or regretting past events. If you live your whole life this way, you will never experience the here and now the way it was meant to be. As an exercise, take a moment *right now* to breathe deeply and look around you. Mentally make a verbal list of everything you see, and identify the things you like. Maybe there are some pretty flowers on your windowsill, or maybe there's a song playing on the radio that you like. The point is to take notice of the world around you *right now* and give thanks for the things in it that make you happy. This is what Eckhart Tolle means when he says you should focus on the power of "here" and "now".

- **Learn to slow things down.** There's no need to accomplish everything as fast as possible. When people start off trying to make schedules and set goals, it can be easy for them to try accomplishing as much as possible within a short period of time. This can quickly cause us to get bogged down and feel like we're not accomplishing anything at all. I have been guilty of this in the past, just like anybody else. I constantly feel like I'm falling behind and somehow need to "catch up" with my peers and the world around me. I found it helpful to take 5 minutes every day and try to be grateful for the things I have in my life, such as my family, a roof over my head, my health, living in the first world, or any number of things. When I do this, it makes me realize how lucky I am and teaches me to appreciate the things I have to be grateful for.

- **Keep a journal.** Start writing down your

thoughts and feelings once a day, and reading them back to yourself to reflect on your own thoughts. Many people would be surprised to learn how little time they spend examining their own thoughts and feelings. You can even keep different journals for different things like personal emotions versus events that happen at work or ideas you had while engaging in one of your hobbies. Your journal can be about whatever you like. It can be about your day, what's been happening in the world recently, your goals, or anything you find helpful to write about. I use journals to write down things I'm grateful for or positive experiences that happen in my day-to-day life. This could be something as simple as somebody holding open a door for me or having a good conversation with an old friend.

- **Meditate.** Sit down in a comfortable position somewhere that you won't be disturbed. Close your eyes and slowly begin to breathe in and out. Try to inhale for four seconds, hold for four seconds, and then exhale for four seconds.

Rinse and repeat. As you slow your breathing, try to empty your mind and be aware of the simple sensations of the world around you. After a while, you will be able to breathe like this without trying, and your mind will naturally reach a calm and collected state. It's a good idea to start slow, and meditate for 5 minutes at a time, gradually increasing your time each day. There are also tons of apps out there that can help with meditation, such as Headspace, or Simple Habit. These apps help you to relax and be in the moment, as well as with guided meditation for different occasions like taking a break, while eating, going for a walk, or many different activities.

- **Exercise your body, not just your fingers.** Exercising your body is an essential part of feeling healthy and able to live your life. Regularly moving around and doing things keeps your juices moving, and has a physiological effect on the way you feel day-to-day. Looking up a simple body weight exercise routine for beginners, or trying out some basic yoga is a good way to start getting exercise. Going for regular walks is another easy way to keep the juices flowing.

You should aim to exercise for at least 30 minutes each day. Too much sitting or standing can be very bad for your health. It should be easy to find time to exercise each day if you have been cutting down on your social media. If you haven't exercised in a while, it's probably a good idea to start slow and gradually work your way up to being as consistent as possible. Don't worry if you don't want to go to the gym or lift weights; there are many different forms of exercise. What's important is choosing something that you can enjoy that gets your heart rate up. You can work out by yourself or join a class if that's more your speed. Some good examples of exercises include:

- ○ Resistance training. This is a form of training where you introduce external resistance and try to work against it. This can be anything from wimple free weights to resistance bands or even your own body weight. Starting with something simple, such as push-ups, is a good idea for beginners.

○ Cardio. Anything that gets your heart pumping is cardio. Examples include running, walking, or swimming. Running or walking is good if you like the outdoors; swimming is good if you have bad knees and need something less high-impact.

○ Pilates. This is a form of low-impact exercise that works on strengthening muscles while improving your posture and flexibility. Trying a class or checking out videos on YouTube is a good place to start.

○ Swimming. Swimming is one of the best exercises you can do, as it works out the entire body without putting too much strain on any single part.

○ Yoga. Yoga focuses on breathing while stretching the body to improve your flexibility and well-being.

○ Dancing. This can be anything from simple ballroom dancing to complex professional ballet. Dancing can be fairly high-impact, so it's a good idea to start slow at first.

- ○ Tai chi. Tai chi is a Chinese martial art focused around fluid movements and breathing to stimulate blood flow. Simple routines to start can be found on YouTube.

I personally split my week in to three sections. I do 3 days of resistance training with exercise bands, and then three days of yoga and walking. I also try to attend a tai chi class once a week when it is available.

- **Build a routine.** All of this scheduling, goal-setting, and habit forming will be useless if your routine doesn't change. After doing these exercises for a while, you *should* find yourself automatically getting into the groove of things. If not, try to brainstorm a routine that incorporates all the strategies that you use from this book. Forming a routine is the easiest way to rehabilitate your habits and expectation.

A good example of an effective daily routine would be as follows:

- ○ Wake up, have a glass of water.

- ○ Meditate for 10-15 minutes.

- Do a 30 minute workout.

- Have a healthy breakfast (preferably home-cooked)

- Get to work; remembering to take regular breaks.

- Take a longer break to eat your lunch, maybe meditate for 5-10 minutes, and then get back to work.

- Stop working when the day is done, leave some time to do important tasks like checking your email or responding to clients.

- Do something relaxing after work, review your goals, take some time to talk to your family or close friends.

- Eat a healthy dinner.

- If you want to engage in social media or something like Netflix, reward yourself by taking some time now to do it. Try not to get trapped and spend too long browsing.

- Do something relaxing before bed in order

to sleep better.

- **Find stimulating hobbies.** It's easier to spend less time on social media if you have something more enjoyable and fulfilling to do instead. Pick up a book, start learning an instrument, download <u>Duolingo</u> and start learning a new language. Go out and ride your bike. Build some model planes. Anything is fine as long as you find it enjoyable and fulfilling.

45 things to do instead of social media

If you're super uncreative and can't think of productive things to do rather than browse Instagram all day, here's a nifty list to get your brain kick started on brainstorming new hobbies. This list is hardly exhaustive; it is simply meant to get the ball rolling thinking of new and exciting things you can do:

- Start practising yoga
- Do tai chi
- Go outside and talk to a stranger once a day
- Visit a new place in your city once a day
- Write a book
- Learn how to cook a new dish
- Learn a new dance (YouTube is your friend)
- Join a class
- Learn a new language
- Start practicing calligraphy
- Ride a bike
- Find local sports clubs to join

- Check out local activist groups

- Attend private movie showings at universities or events

- Start a collection of non-fiction books

- Study the history of the Roman Empire

- Try out metal working

- Start doing arts and crafts

- Try out canvas painting

- Try some photography (you can start with just your phone!)

- Start a business

- Start doing freelance work in your spare time

- Learn to build PCs

- Write a poem

- Write a letter to the editor of your local newspaper

- Join a church group

- Volunteer at a soup kitchen

- Clean your room

- Go fishing
- Learn to fly a plane (this is surprisingly affordable)
- Try fencing
- Practice martial arts (boxing is a good place to start)
- Learn about fashion
- Learn how to style hair
- Learn how to garden
- Mow your lawn
- Learn how to make candy
- Learn how to bake
- Write a letter to your state representative
- Start paying attention to politics
- Read up on history in general
- Go for a mani/pedi or a facial
- Get a haircut
- Try doodling and/or sketching
- Check out new businesses in your area

- Learn about the stock market

Fulfillment exercise

Right now, *yes now!* Take out a pen and paper. Write down three different activities that you could do this month. Once you've come up with three activities, narrow it down to the one you want to do the most.

Then, break that thing down into workable goals. Write down the first step you will take towards making this goal a reality. Now, write down something like: *for the next thirty days, I will _____.*

This exercise will teach you what it feels like to work toward a goal that is important to you. It will make you feel like the things that you want are achievable rather than impossible.

Summary

- **Do a 30 day detox.** Staying away from social media for 30 days will teach your brain to rely less on the validation it gets from checking your phone or computer. If you have trouble with 30 days, try a shorter period of time.

- **Deep work.** Humans have a built-in mechanism for being focused on their work. Learn to tap into this energy and feel what it means to truly be focused on a task.

- **It's okay to be bored.** Boredom is a natural state of the human mind that drives us to accomplish things. Don't simply appease your boredom by engaging with instant gratification.

- **Find time for yourself.** If you spend all your time working hard towards your goals or somebody else's goals, you will never feel like you're getting anything out of your life. Set aside time to spend reflecting and doing things you want to do.

- **Live in the moment.** Don't spend all of your time worrying about the past and the future.

Learn to give thanks for the way the world is in the here and now.

- **Learn to slow down.** There's no need to accomplish all of your goals right away. Learning to slow down and take things at your own pace is essential to leading a fulfilling life.

- **Keep a journal.** Writing down your ideas and feelings can help you reflect on how you can improve, or identify areas of your life that require improvement.

- **Meditate.** Take time to breathe slowly, and be mindful of the world around you. Practice rhythmic breathing and try to empty your mind once in a while.

- **Exercise.** You have to work out more than just your fingers. Forming an exercise routine will help you keep the juices flowing.

- **Routine.** By now, you should be forming new habits around the various exercises we've been discussing. Try to form a routine so that your body and mind can get into the groove of being mindful and more fulfilled.

- **Start new hobbies.** If you have things you enjoy more than social media, you will spend less time wasting away on Instagram or Twitter.

- **Do things other than social media.** Form habits and find new hobbies outside of the internet. Try to think of new and exciting things that you've always wanted to do, and use your extra time to start pursuing those goals!

For the final chapter, we'll be going over what we've learned, as well as reviewing different materials and resources we can use to learn more or help us along our journey.

Chapter 7: Final thoughts

Addiction and dysfunction have become commonplace for many people in the world today. The devices and digital services that were supposed to make our lives easier and more convenient have quickly evolved into a way for developers and companies to waste our time and money. Many people forget how fulfilling it can be to actually get out and enjoy your life.

That's why I'm happy for *you* in this moment. Taking control of your digital life is an essential step to making yourself feel fulfilled with your life. Most people don't realize how much their digital habits can bog them down and detach them from natural feelings of happiness, but *you* are willing to take the steps and do what needs to be done.

Keep making those lists, and keep researching new apps to make yourself more efficient. Set yourself up for success by building new habits and giving yourself a fighting chance. Let other people in your life know what worked for you, so you can share these tips and habits with them. Building up your relationships with those around you whom you value is one of the best ways to give yourself a fighting chance.

Before we say goodbye, let's review what we've learned one last time. Many of the things we've learned (such as organizing your email) will need to be done regularly to have any effect.

Summary and Action plan

- Create a system for organizing your computer

- Organize important photos or photos for clients (use an appropriate system)

- Do the same for your video files (consider getting an external hard drive for storing important files)

- Organize your music; consider using a streaming service such as Spotify or YouTube

- Disable or remove unnecessary extensions from your browser

- Use apps and extensions to stay focused

- Use tags, rules, and labels to organize your email inbox

- Learn to be concise when responding to emails

- Limit your email time to certain periods (twice a day works well)

- Create templates for repetitive responses

- Unsubscribe from newsletters and spam accounts

- Limit your social media time to a small amount of time after your work is done

- Use apps to reduce your screen time

- Try a 30-day digital detox

- Start keeping a journal

- Try meditation, or yoga, or tai chi

- Start exercising

- Find stimulating hobbies

- Get out and enjoy your life!

"If you want to swim, jump into the water. On dry land, no frame of mind is going to help you."

-Bruce Lee

Resources

- IoBit Uninstaller

- StayFocused

- WasteNoTime

- Digital Wellbeing

- OffTime

- Moment

- Flipd

- Freedom

- Appblock

- Selfcontrol

- Trello

- Evernote

- Todoist

Further Reading

The Art of Decluttering and Organizing

How to Tidy Up your Home, Stop Clutter, and Simplify your Life (Without Going Crazy)

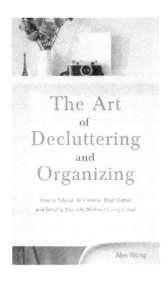

https://bit.ly/artofdecluttering1

The Decluttering Your Life Workbook

The Secrets of Organizing Your Home, Mind, Health, Finances, and Relationships in 6 Easy Steps

https://bit.ly/declutteryourlife1

Review Request

If you enjoyed this guide or found it useful...

I'd like to ask you for a quick favor:

Please share your thoughts and leave a quick REVIEW. Your feedback matters and helps me to make improvements so I can provide the best content possible.

Reviews are incredibly helpful to both readers and authors, like me, so any help would be greatly appreciated.

Thank you!

Pretty Please...

If you enjoyed this book and picked up some tips and ideas from it, would you consider letting others know about it?

Here are some easy ways you can do this:

Leave a review on Amazon.

Leave a review on Goodreads.

Share it on your favorite social media sites like Facebook, Twitter, or Instagram.

Tell your friends, family members, and colleagues about it.

Thanks again for your support. You RULE!

Sincerely

Alex Wong

About the Author

Alex Wong is a professional writer and content strategist. He's also the head copywriter for an advertising media agency specializing in custom websites and internet marketing. He's the first person in his family to graduate from university, earning himself a degree in psychology. Alex is the author of several best-selling books published on Amazon. One of his main influences in life is Bruce Lee, who taught him, "The more we value things, the less we value ourselves."

Growing up with a hoarder in the house was very difficult on Alex. Thankfully, he was able to turn this negative experience into a positive. Once he embraced minimalism, he was able to transform his personal and professional life. Now he's striving to help others declutter, get organized and improve their lives.

Check out Alex's other books here:

https://bit.ly/alexwong-books1

Do you need help with your writing, content or marketing? Would you like to get in touch?

Email Alex: alex@alexwongpublishing.com

Or learn more here:

https://alexwongpublishing.com/

CPSIA information can be obtained
at www.ICGtesting.com
Printed in the USA
BVHW041122090521
606888BV00019B/2334

9 781774 870006